T0355142

The Ethics of Architecture

ETHICS IN CONTEXT

Series Editor
Markus D. Dubber
Professor of Law and Director, Centre for Ethics
University of Toronto

Published under the auspices of the Centre for Ethics, University of
Toronto, Ethics in Context explores the ethical dimensions of interesting,
provocative, and timely questions. Books in the series are accessible, yet
provide something rigorous that stimulates thought and debate, in keeping
with the interdisciplinary and inclusive vision that animates the Centre for
Ethics at the interface between academic research and public discourse.

The Ethics
of Architecture

Mark Kingwell

Department of Philosophy
University of Toronto

OXFORD
UNIVERSITY PRESS

Oxford University Press is a department of the University of Oxford. It furthers the University's objective of excellence in research, scholarship, and education by publishing worldwide. Oxford is a registered trade mark of Oxford University Press in the UK and certain other countries.

Published in the United States of America by Oxford University Press
198 Madison Avenue, New York, NY 10016, United States of America.

Library of Congress Cataloging-in-Publication Data
Names: Kingwell, Mark, 1963– author.
Title: The ethics of architecture / Mark Kingwell, Department of Philosophy, University of Toronto.
Description: New York, NY : Oxford University Press, 2021. | Includes bibliographical references and index.
Identifiers: LCCN 2020039408 (print) | LCCN 2020039409 (ebook) | ISBN 9780197558546 (hardback) |
  ISBN 9780197558560 (epub) | ISBN 9780197558553 (updf) | ISBN 9780197558577 (digital-online)
Subjects: LCSH: Architecture—Philosophy. | Architecture—Moral and ethical aspects.
Classification: LCC NA2500 .K49 2020 (print) | LCC NA2500 (ebook) | DDC 720.1—dc23
LC record available at https://lccn.loc.gov/2020039408
LC ebook record available at https://lccn.loc.gov/2020039409

DOI: 10.1093/oso/9780197558546.001.0001

1 3 5 7 9 8 6 4 2

Printed by Sheridan Books, Inc., United States of America

Note to Readers
This publication is designed to provide accurate and authoritative information in regard to the subject matter covered. It is based upon sources believed to be accurate and reliable and is intended to be current as of the time it was written. It is sold with the understanding that the publisher is not engaged in rendering legal, accounting, or other professional services. If legal advice or other expert assistance is required, the services of a competent professional person should be sought. Also, to confirm that the information has not been affected or changed by recent developments, traditional legal research techniques should be used, including checking primary sources where appropriate.

(Based on the Declaration of Principles jointly adopted by a Committee of the American Bar Association and a Committee of Publishers and Associations.)

You may order this or any other Oxford University Press publication
by visiting the Oxford University Press website at www.oup.com.

Contents

"Without Architecture"
There would have to be another vision for occupying space,
new rituals for sitting and standing, for the physical interruption
of the planar world. No longer would we distinguish
between *exist* and *inhabit*. No asking where we live.

We live. Now to lug our dwellings like a hermit crab
or not. What would the word for *shelter* be?
Like *cave* or *under-hang*, or more like *shade* or *company*?
Two hundred words for *horizon* comprise an anthem.

Without walls, privacy would still occur, only wilder.
We would vote by standing upright, and emphasize
ourselves by raising our hands, lengthening our votes
as a challenge to the levelness of the meeting place.

Prisons would be nothing—but banishment theoretical and severe:
how best to find a cave or shade beyond the vanishing point?
And who goes there? It was the heretic and prodigy who said:
I can make a cathedral of my condition and worship there.
                    — Paul Vermeersch, from *Self Defence for the Brave and
                         Happy: Poems* (Toronto: ECW Press, 2018)

                              * * *

"Being human is itself difficult, and therefore all kinds of
settlements (except dream cities) have problems. Big cities
have difficulties in abundance, because they have people in
abundance."
     — Jane Jacobs, from *The Death and Life of Great American
                  Cities* (New York: Random House, 1961)

Preface: Plague Cities of the Future

Some years ago I wrote a book about millennial anxiety that concluded with an affectionate description of the Canadian city, Winnipeg, where I spent seven years of my life before heading off to college. Recalling the annual waves of floods, blizzards, tent-caterpillar infestations, and summer hailstorms that battered trees and cars into failure, I labeled the town known officially as "The Gateway to the West" as "Plague City." It is indeed a bleak and forbidding place, where the sidewalks crack from deep winter cold snaps and summer seems to last about a month. Not surprisingly, its long-time residents are resilient, friendly, and cooperative. They look out for each other. The rest of us take the first viable opportunity to move somewhere less hostile to human existence.

The year 2020 has seen most of the world's cities transformed with startling swiftness into new versions of a genuine Plague City, not just a Midwestern town beset by routine environmental events. The novel coronavirus outbreak that likely started in wet markets in China spread with deadly speed and virulence across the planet, creating global pandemic conditions unprecedented in human history, even including the 1918 Spanish Flu, the 1665 Great Plague, or the Black Death. The final death tolls may prove smaller than those world-historical crises—one hopes substantially smaller—but the overall social and economic effects are larger, and will continue longer, than anything the world has witnessed before.

I had just completed the main manuscript of this book when news of the virus and its wildfire COVID-19 infections were beginning to take hold in mainstream consciousness. Everyone will recall that there was a period of six weeks or more, roughly all of February and at least half of March 2020, when most North Americans and many Europeans acted as if the virus was containable, and hence ignorable, in the same way that earlier SARS and MERS outbreaks had been. There was a sense that extreme measures were unwarranted if not hysterical, and some commentators insisted the disease was less worrisome than the annual flu. By early April, of course, the world had decisively and permanently changed. As the first weeks of social distancing and lockdowns grew into months, it became clear that nothing in our world would ever be the same.

This is especially evident in cities, where more than half of the world's population currently resides, a figure estimated to rise to more than two-thirds of the total global population within thirty years. Once jammed city streets were, almost overnight, stripped of all traffic except delivery vehicles and stunt-speeding joyriders risking tickets for the chance to unleash on open concrete. Sidewalks, once among the clearest signs of urban health when filled with jostling shoppers, cafés, and bars, became zones of proximity suspicion and long queues of frustrated citizens in search of groceries or liquor. The household threshold, always a bulwark of privacy and security, was now a kind of virus-proofing airlock, closed to casual visitors and close family members alike. Those of us with the luxury of staying at home—and, despite all the inconveniences and cabin fever, it was a luxury—learned to order our days in a new manner, working to stay productive and hopeful, while maybe also trying not to start in on that hard-won liquor too soon.

There were and are so many stories of the long-term effects of this pandemic that it is futile to catalog them all. What was on my own mind, as I observed changes in my neighborhood and in the virtual space of the Internet (without which, obviously, the psychic costs of self-isolation would have been much greater), were the ethical implications of the virus for everyday life.

Some of these are *general and structural*. Community-wide challenges demand collective response over individual interest. The needs of the few may have to be sacrificed for the well-being of the many. This is obvious, even one does not endorse a strict felicific calculus on the order of Jeremy Bentham's potentially ruthless utilitarianism. You don't have to advocate forced selective sacrifice of some to preserve the comfort of others—the nightmare dystopia of Ursula Le Guin's "The Ones Who Walk Away from Omelas"—to accept that luxury goods like restaurant meals, easy air travel, and baseball games may become dispensable when overall public health is at stake.

Nevertheless, this basic logic of collective sharing of the health burden caused bristles as the weeks turned into months. We in the developed world have been steeped in an ideology of liberal individualism that does not always mesh well with other-oriented sacrifice. There are also, depending on political context, currents of anti-authoritarian or even scofflaw sentiment running beneath general norms of civility and cooperation. Competitive advantage is not curbed by sentiments about the vulnerable; quasi-Darwinian and Malthusian ideas of "population-correction" continued to swirl.

Couple this with the exposed social fault lines of life and we witnessed disturbing realities. Viruses are thought be indiscriminate in their visitation of disease and death, but of course this was not the case. Populations experienced the ravages of the virus in uneven ways: the elderly, the poor, in the United States the Black population all suffered far worse disproportionate effects of the spread. That these facts were linked to underlying social and economic conditions somehow did not halt the relentless advance of neoliberal ideology, the twisted child of individualism, whereby all suffering is somehow the victim's responsibility. Yes, those sick and dying should have had the foresight to be born wealthier, whiter, and better educated.

There is then a deeper level of what might be called *specific and existential* ethical challenges. As boredom and anxiety rose, for example, even unto the most economically privileged, crises of loneliness and despair began to loom. Mental illness, or simply stress, is an inevitable byproduct of fast and comprehensive change in life patterns. And not all coping mechanisms are solutions better than the problem itself. Some of us found philosophical reflection in our boredom, a source of possible wisdom and perhaps an altered sense of time and expectation. Value scales were revised, the seemingly crucial concerns of work or social appearance relegated to a lower status, the worth of connection and fortitude, of radical hope beyond concrete short-term optimism, elevated.

At the same time, reflexive desires for a "return to normal" were serially revealed as unworkable, dark dreams of what were in fact the yawning injustices and planetary dangers of that pre-pandemic fantasyland of privilege. The exclusive fortress of prosperity, in some places literally walled against incursion from without, was shown to be a house of cards where a tiny minority experienced entitlements so invisible to self-reflection that we had, even before, made a joke of so-called "First World Problems"—which were, to many, still seen as actual *problems* in need of solution, usually involving money and stronger gates both physical and social.

The structural and the existential dimensions of ethics are linked, to be sure, and the latter can help limn the contours of the former. Even so, one clear insight from these first weeks of ethical challenge, pandemic-style, was the old lesson that reflection is itself a luxury good. When you are fighting for your life or livelihood, there is no time for boredom or even for thoughts about time. There is no experience of time at all, if by that we mean a feeling of projection or possibility rather than grinding duration. There is just the ever-present, ever-renewing moment of struggle: the image of Sisyphus permanently on the hillside, and not enjoying the happiness that Albert Camus alleged for him.

For the rest of us, this has been an opportunity, not always taken up, to think hard about what we have done and what we might do. The backbone of ethical life is the possibility, even if somehow fictional or delusional, of human continuity. Responsibility means nothing if consequences are not tied to actions, if past selves are not held accountable to future iterations of them. Extreme philosophical thought might dispute this temporal stringing of selfhood, and with good reason, but we cannot live our everyday lives without it. I must assume, even if fundamentally unjustifiable, a connection between who I was yesterday, who I am today, and who I will be tomorrow.

* * *

Every human undertaking, certainly every profession, likewise relies on such necessary fictions of future realities hinged to present and past. Architecture is no exception, and indeed given its fundamental

project of building—an activity that is inherently future-oriented—
it provides a clear exemplar of human belief in continuity. From the
most temporary hut or tent in which to shelter for a night, to a temple
meant to last a thousand years and more, *to build is to believe*: in survival, in protection, in shared aspiration, even when possible in the
lasting but variable quality of beauty.

As we all watched our built environments altered metaphysically
by the COVID-19 pandemic, the concrete, stone steel, and glass apparently unchanged and yet decisively altered, I kept thinking about
what the emergent new world would mean for the ethics of architecture. I asked an architect friend of mine, who was as it happens the
last person I met physically for a drink in a downtown bar before the
social restrictions and closures altered daily life decisively in March
2020. "My expectation is that the topic will be more relevant in that
world than it would have been otherwise. I'm used to spending almost all of my time mentally in the near future and I think most of
the people I spend my days with do the same thing. This experience,
the isolation and the uncertainty about what's to come, has really
snapped the lot of us into the present. I think one of the consequences
of that is a heightened awareness of one's physical environment, the
built environment, your community. There's something paradoxical
about that when we're breaking the Internet with all of the virtual
meetings and hangouts. Nonetheless, a global population emerging
from some medium-term house arrest seems like a pretty fertile audience for reflection on the ethics of architecture." I believe he may
be right but, as with all other aspects of the new pandemic world, it is
impossible to predict accurately.

What we do know, from past experience, is that architecture and
design have regularly been fundamentally directed and altered
by world-historical events, including wars, plagues, famines, and
pestilence. The specter of the atomic bomb drove not only a miniature industry of bomb-shelter design and underground-bunker
military installations but, more obviously and inescapably, the vast
interconnections of the Eisenhower Interstate Highway System.
Authorized by the Federal Aid Highway Act of 1956, this brainchild
of the U.S. President and former Supreme Commander of Allied

Forces in Europe during the Second World War, was inspired in part by the *Reichsautobahn* system, which then-General Eisenhower recognized as essential to national defense and the free movement of troops and matériel in times of crisis or war.

On a smaller scale, the terrorist attacks of September 11, 2001—whose total death toll was surpassed by COVID-19 late in March 2020—reset security and construction protocols throughout the United States, especially in public places. The American death toll then surpassed that of the Vietnam, Afghanistan, and Iraq Wars combined by late April, accounting for a quarter of the reported global total. Not a great deal of actual design was immediately changed as a result of these numbers, to be sure; indeed, there was only passing mention of the deaths, and no official federal recognition of mourning, such as lowered flags. Rather, it was our ways of occupying public spaces that was shifted. Security checks and the presence of armed agents of the state, not to mention growing camera-cover surveillance in most parts of big cities, themselves became design features of the built environment—to the point that surveillance itself was a kind of architectural element, built into new projects as much as HVAC systems or the choice of glass friendly to migrating birds.

Going back further, one think of numerous examples that shaped building styles and occupation patterns over the centuries: the revolutionary ferment, crime, bad sanitation, and overcrowding in Paris that enabled Baron von Haussmann to transform the City of Light into spiraling *arrondissements*, wide boulevards, and broad parks or forests for the benefit of citizens and air quality alike. One cannot imagine the structure of medieval cities absent the forced migration of countryside peasants seeking shelter, food, and stimulus away from the uncertain depredations of isolated life. Public squares and temples, open marketplaces and boardwalks, sweeping Georgian crescents or narrow Edinburgh granite towers—every familiar feature of architecture is an answer to prevailing social, cultural, and economic conditions.

We can ever survey the fictional depictions of plague conditions for insight here. The three most-often mentioned books in the first months of 2020's pandemic were Giovanni Boccaccio's *The Decameron* (It., *Decamerone*, 1353), Daniel Defoe's *A Journal of the Plague Year* (1722), and Albert Camus's *The Plague* (Fr., *La Peste*, 1947). Each of these was plumbed for its lessons about living with, and through, a pandemic. There was much to learn in all three cases, but little attention was given to the architectural aspects of the scenes unfolded in narrative.

The most striking thing about *The Decameron*, for example, is that its framing story is of a group of young aristocrats who repair to a country estate to avoid the worst ravages on the Black Death in their city. This privilege, not unlike the frowned-upon flight of wealthy urbanites to country cottages in the spring of 2020, provides the enabling conditions for the series of ten tales that then unfold. Defoe's *Journal*, presented as an eyewitness account of the Great London Plague of 1665 (a millenarian milestone: a thousand years plus the mark of Satan), is detailed in its description of Whitechapel streets, houses, and intersections. Camus's story, meanwhile, is inseparable from its setting in an Algerian city, perhaps based on Oran, that has suffered waves of disease affecting residents and vacationers, rich and poor, in varying ways depending upon their manner of occupying the crowded Arab quarter or the more salubrious districts.

One could multiply the examples to include more recent novels such as Timothy Findley's brilliant but neglected *Headhunter* (1993), in which a starling-borne deadly plague called *sturnusemia* is traced through the posh homes, back alleys, public libraries, university quads, and tangled ravines of downtown Toronto. The book contains this passage, near its beginning, that will haunt our memories of early 2020:

> Somehow, there seemed to be a secondary plague on the loose—one of non-belief. *This is not happening*, people said—*this is not plausible. We will wait for an acceptable explanation.* And yet, though no other explanation had been forthcoming, and even in spite of the mounting death toll, the population at large gave every indication of ignoring the threat of sturnusemia. . . . Many were bored with what they claimed were *scare tactics*. Most were skeptical—others were incredulous. A very few

believed—but neither belief nor incredulity prevented the disease from claiming its victims.[1]

The disease does not care what you believe. And then, some pages later, there is this detail:

> Because of [the contagion], there was a roaring trade in surgical masks for those who could make their way to stores and hospitals. But, in time, the supplies ran out and the people reverted to old-west style—a city of frontier bandits done up in red and blue bandannas.[2]

Yes indeed: the everyday bandits of pandemic and plague, those ordinary robbers of complacency and comfort . . .

In all of these cases and more, the architectural contours of the city are themselves *part of the plague condition*. They sculpt and steer responses and attitudes, mold behavior and reaction. So much is obvious. What then, do current conditions mean for the cities of the future? What design principles will have to be abandoned, what news ones adopted, and what may the ethical implications of these choices amount to? In the short term, we walked down the middle of empty streets and skirted other dog walkers in parks, shuffled along in our queues, and answered the door only after the delivery person had left. What part of these changes, and what others, will prevail in the longer span of time?

The proximate answer, I think, concerns once-dominant ideas of public life, especially in cities. For decades, many planners and architects have been devoted to visions of urban existence modeled, or at least partly influenced, by the Jane Jacobs school of thought. Which is to say: small scale, mixed use, significant density, thriving street life, pedestrian priority, and the celebration of public transit and sometimes bicycles over automobile traffic. The legendary battle between Jacobs and New York Über-Planner Robert Moses captures the stakes, albeit often with caricature rather than nuance. The preservation of Washington Square Park over the planned downtown extension of Fifth Avenue is a symbolic but also material synecdoche for a clash of urban philosophies.

But some tenets of the Jacobs vision are no longer viable. Public transit, already viewed as undesirable, may never rebound, even when people no longer routinely fear infection through proximity. Downtown density may be unavoidable in working life, but stay-at-home labor will likely empty out once-full office towers the way the Empire State Building was systematically vacated in the post-war 1950s.[3] The hard-won revitalization of residential downtowns may give way to new waves of white flight to the widely spaced, car-friendly suburbs, where grocery shopping can be done in vast uncrowded big-box stores and cars can enter garages with a direct door into the living space. Already in the spring of 2020, critics began to note how 1960s high-rise residential developments on the Corbusian Radiant City model, formerly reviled for their creation of ground-level crime zones and vertical ghettos, were now *in addition* overcrowded viral hotspots, dense with disease along narrow hallways and in elevators.[4] At the same time, some urbanists insisted that we not blame density itself, and high-rises in particular, for the spread of the virus, as writers from New York to Minneapolis to Vancouver had done, blaming "New Urbanist overlords" for the contagion.[5] One analysis, of Oscar Niemeyer's Edifício Copan apartment complex in São Paulo, the densest pocket in the country with more than 5,000 residents in one block—also a building mentioned later in this book—noted that social distancing and collective action had largely stopped the virus. This is a real success amid the bizarre denial-rhetoric of Brazilian President Jair Bolsonaro.[6]

Whatever one's views on high-rise residential developments, ex-urban sprawl, once the enemy of all right-thinking planners, may prove the solution for a frightened populace—or that portion of it wealthy enough to afford isolation. We will see less Manhattan, and more Los Angeles.

The authors of a *New York Times* feature on the future of post-pandemic cities put it this way: "The pandemic has been particularly devastating to America's biggest cities, as the virus has found fertile ground in the density that is otherwise prized. And it comes as the country's major urban centers were already losing their appeal for many Americans, as skyrocketing rents and changes in the labor market have pushed the country's youngest adults to suburbs and smaller cities often far from the coasts."[7] That was published on April 19, 2020, even before the largest effects could be registered.

* * *

Cities have often been modeled intellectually as layers of circulation and transaction: the endless movements of heat and cold; of people and their desires; of money and its objects; of food and waste; of materials and designs; and so on. These circulatory systems, some clearly physical, others more ephemeral or metaphorical, have been severely disrupted by new environmental conditions. The long tail of effects on the very idea of the city, and of buildings within it, will not abate for some decades, if ever.

The architecture critic Oliver Wainwright pointed out that disease has long been a feature of basic design:

> From antibacterial brass doorknobs to broad, well-ventilated boulevards, our cities and buildings have always been shaped by disease. It was cholera that influenced the modern street grid, as 19th-century epidemics prompted the introduction of sewage systems that required the roads above them to be wider and straighter, along with new zoning laws to prevent overcrowding.
>
> The third plague pandemic, a bubonic outbreak that began in China in 1855, changed the design of everything from drainpipes to door thresholds and building foundations, in the global war against the rat. And the wipe-clean aesthetic of modernism was partly a result of tuberculosis, with light-flooded sanatoriums inspiring an era of white-painted rooms, hygienic tiled bathrooms and the ubiquitous mid-century recliner chair. Form has always followed fear of infection, just as much as function.[8]

This apt summary, as well as reminding us of some hidden lessons of history, highlights what is very likely to change in architecture as a direct function of the COVID-19 pandemic.[9]

Bars and restaurants will disappear or be comprehensively altered into semi-isolated gathering zones, perhaps demanding remote ordering and service. Parks, walkways, and pedestrian zones will continue to be governed by suspicion and the remnants, whether officially mandated or not, of social distancing. The measures of so-called defensive architecture, already in place in many cities, will be expanded. Bars on park benches to discourage lying down; metal spikes beneath highway overpasses to prevent camping out; cow-gate barriers on parks to control access: these features of urban architecture are already with us. It is easily conceivable that planning commissions, clients, and calls for proposals will include such things, and more, to minimize contact between persons. More and more preventive internal features will be demanded by clients: full-wall display screens, isolated-office uplinks, private or limited-access elevators.

Designers will also need to incorporate public-health mechanisms within their plans. The widely spaced hand sanitizers of yesterday will be supplanted by temperature stations, testing pods, perhaps full-body scanners. Security checks will be operationalized to validate immunity credentials, the way they now do for sharp objects and fluids. Large public buildings—airports, government offices, stadiums, and theaters—will need to redesigned with ongoing social distancing in mind: widely spaced seating, long security and health-check corridors, remote delivery of concessions or forms. It may even be the case that large public gatherings will be banned or, if not that, looked upon with misgiving and so allowed to fall into nonexistence.

In addition to airlock-style entry and exit thresholds already noted, residential housing will likewise demand more boredom-repelling virtual features and connections, plus floor plans that facilitate possible future quarantine or isolation. Outside spaces, from porches and lanais to gardens and open public expanses, will need to be rethought comprehensively. Testing pods will be established at the controlled entrances to parks and common fields. Policing, whether in-person or on-camera, will be constant in such spaces, to punish noncompliance. Ticketing of distancing violations will soon prove to be a municipal revenue stream greater than old-fashioned speeding tickets and parking fines.

All of this will exacerbate existing socioeconomic divisions, and create new ones based on access to testing, vaccination, and ongoing reliable healthcare. Our ideas of public and private, already widely contested or just misunderstood, will suffer further conceptual erosion. Privacy, which had become a species of luxury goods under former conditions, will be elevated into preserves enjoyed only by the hyper-rich, even as public space will cease to mean anything good, rather a kind of presumptive death sentence. Visionaries of architecture and urban planning often speaking of utopian and dystopian futures as if they operated as a binary function: it is either *Nineteen Eighty-Four* or it is *Brave New World*. The reality is that it is always both at once, and one person's nightmare city is another person's endless playground.

How will architects cope under these emergent conditions? All the ethical quandaries that are outlined in the pages that follow will remain. Some will be ramped up, to the point of dilemma or even self-betrayal. Can you design to specifications that you know are unjust to the many in the service of the few? Can you facilitate safety features that work only to further inequalities and even lead to shunning or punishment of violators? Or are there nimble compromises to be executed here, the usual massaging of clients toward better choices? The challenges posed by pandemic and post-pandemic reality will be as grave for future architects as environmental responsibility, social justice, and the reach of artificial intelligence are for present ones.

Like many of us, I would like to think that this moment of forced reflection, this pause in the reckless velocities of neoliberal life, will indeed offer a respite from the relentless near-future thinking of most architectural practice, and also that the pages that follow may be of some in that reflection. We cannot help but project our thoughts and plans into the future, yet we can only act in the present. The event horizons of designing and planning are variable, but they are not otherworldly. If the long-term vistas right now seem bleak—and they do—there are nevertheless many things we can do to shift them: as citizens, as architects, and as all those whom the built environment affects and affords.

Architecture has ever been a struggle between human aspiration and the material conditions of the various environments that encompass the biosphere. Our desires must follow that path of improvement, not acquiescence, and the journey must begin right here, right now. The city of the future, plague or no plague, is and always will be built by us. There is, after all, nobody else.

Built Forms and Ethics: The General Issues

One commentator has argued, persuasively, that it is a story about "everything that is wrong with architecture."[1] It defends and maybe inspires a form of "morality" that permits its "dictatorial protagonist" to commit "architectural terrorism." It is the most notorious fiction ever written about architecture, and especially about architecture and ethics.

I first read Ayn Rand's 1943 novel *The Fountainhead* when I was fifteen years old. This may be the optimal age for a reader of this ponderous tome, especially an adolescent male with grand creative ideas about construction and city-building but no outlets for them except designing graph-paper levels of tortuous adventure for an ongoing *Dungeons & Dragons* game or gluing together elaborate polystyrene replicas of airships and assault vehicles.

The latter pursuit could be expanded into what was then known as "kit-bashing," where elements of a few preset model designs could be repurposed to enable outlandish science-fictional hybrids—jet-powered dinosaurs, flying tanks, undersea cars—but these always somehow fell short of imagination's pull. Nobody I knew could, for example, come close to the transcendental modeling abilities of Gerry and Sylvia Anderson, who created the "SuperMarionation" television and film franchises *Captain Scarlet* and *Thunderbirds Are Go!* (both mid-1960s). In these miniaturized worlds created on tiny sets, whole futuristic cities came to life under the narrative guidance of Martian invasion or global safety crisis. The models visible on the shows could then be purchased as die-cast treasures.

The Ethics of Architecture. Mark Kingwell, Oxford University Press (2021). © Mark Kingwell.
DOI: 10.1093/oso/9780197558546.003.0001

Even the actual architectural toys then available, in particular a fiendishly difficult design-and-build line called *Super City* (Ideal Toys, 1967–68), with sharp plastic modular pieces and tinted-glass inlays, never quite delivered on the promise of making something in the world that translated vision into concrete reality. Bought for me and my brothers by our father, this series of kits was like some engineer's version of what happens when people graduate from LEGO—a building kit capable of producing Modernist cities of to-morrow and multiple Sixties-Mod skyscrapers.

As we have seen in the years since, though, not only has LEGO evolved into elaborate by-the-numbers kits that make old airplane models look simplistic and dinky by contrast, but basic LEGO has itself become an artistic and architectural material in its own right, enabling the work of, among others: Ekow Nimako, who uses only black bricks in his sculptures; Raymond Girard, who creates fan-tastical buildings and skylines using only the most basic of playset bricks; and Jan Vormann, who uses standard-issue plastic bricks to fill in and shore up old brick walls.

Artist Douglas Coupland has reflected on both kinds of toys in var-ious publications and exhibitions, noting "the profound effect toys can have—not only on how children learn to perceive the world, but also in terms of the kinds of things they produce as adults." In one bril-liant riff on *Super City*, he annotates the image on the box cover with imagined locations drawn from modish 1960s iconography: Henry Kissinger and Jill St. John having sex, a parking garage that only accepts vehicles with gull-wing doors, Walt Disney's head stored in liquid helium, Karen Carpenter's apartment, a Jarvik heart transplant center, and the Qantas airline headquarters (trivia check: as Dustin Hoffman notes in *Rain Man* [1988, d. Barry Levinson], there were no passenger fatalities on that carrier, the world's safest). A 2005 exhibi-tion at the Canadian Centre for Architecture featured many different kits and notional constructions but also a perfect downsized version of the World Trade Center towers, then still freshly mourned, and the thankfully still-standing CN Tower in Toronto.

Architecture, we might say, is everywhere in the imagination, even if that means the universe of the toy box or false-paneled basement rec room before it is the building site or actual cleared-city footprint. The high drama, or maybe high cheese, of Rand's novel excited the nascent imagination of many a budding architect. I recall a television of the day, Art Garfunkel on the Mike Davis or Dick Cavett shows, explaining that he enrolled in architecture school after reading Rand's feverish paean to individual creative genius. Perhaps luckily for the world, he teamed up with Paul Simon instead.

My brother, already in engineering school, heard me enthuse about Howard Roark and beautiful but emotionally unstable Dominique Francon; wavering Gail Wynand; evil Ellsworth M. Toohey; and above all steadfast, stalwart Howard Roark, servant to no man or system. He suggested architecture might be my own university major. He also argued what is true and better, that architecture combines the best of technical and humane study into a potentially glorious mixture, the most basic of all applied arts.

When I then came to see King Vidor's luscious black-and-white, post-Expressionist film adaptation of the novel (1949), I was, like many viewers, even more fetched by the story. Roark, described in the book as squat, muscular, and red-haired, is stretched into gaunt, stiffly handsome Gary Cooper, the most wooden of matinee idols, a barely moving totem of masculine reticence. Dominique, portrayed by Patricia Neal just twenty-two and at her most sulky, is irresistible. Indeed, the two stars found each other irresistible off the set as well as on, even though Cooper was twenty-five years older.

Their subsequent tumultuous affair nearly ruined his marriage and led to physical abuse—Cooper hit Neal when he thought she was giving in to the predations of rival Kirk Douglas—and a forced abortion of their conceived child. The rape scene that features so disturbingly in both novel and film, when imperious Dominique is made to submit to overpowering Roark and then later admits this was her secret wish, is made even more unpalatable when these tabloid details float to the surface.

But the film has virtues and some moments of unintended humor. Canadian-born actor Raymond Massey, playing the Hell's Kitchen kid made good as newspaper baron Wynand, is creepily charming even in his hypocrisy. The evil Toohey, overplayed hilariously by

Robert Douglas, is the ultimate Rand straw man, a demagogue without scruple, wielding a long cigarette holder held Nazi-style between thumb and forefinger. Maybe best of all is actor Kent Smith as the craven, talentless, brush-cut Peter Keating, a mediocre social climber who depends on Roark's genius for his fragile reputation. When Roark—spoiler alert!—decides to dynamite the public-housing project Keating has allowed to become compromised, we see Rand's basic drama of good and evil played out explosively. (An architect friend of mine once told me that when she was in school, she thought every one of her classmates was a Peter Keating.)

The production design, meanwhile, especially the obvious Frank Lloyd Wright and International Style rip-off building designed by Edward Carrere, are rendered in gorgeous black-and-white stills. Roark's mentor Henry Cameron (Henry Hull) uses his dying words to express the standard Louis Sullivan mantra that "form should follow function," and laments the "popular taste" that dictates modern architects should design buildings that look "like Greek temples, Gothic cathedrals, and mongrels of every ancient style they could borrow."

In one memorable scene, a sleek elevated-base office tower proposed by Roark is "improved" with Doric doodads pasted on post facto by a gang of thuggish neoclassicist lackeys. They are led by Gus Webb, played here by John Doucette, a stocky actor best known for playing hit men, gangsters, cowboys, and sea captains. "Why shouldn't we get to express our creativity?" he snarls, bringing a walking stick swiftly down on Roark's original model. This violent insistence on dead forms seems bleakly funny in the film, but its real-world equivalents might be the tiresome and frankly idiotic architectural meanderings of Britain's Prince Charles, enemy of anything he considers "modern" because, perversely, he is concerned about the future.[2] As a writer in *The Guardian* pointed out, the arguments in favor of "timelessness" are no more than veiled conservative, even reactionary forays.

And so, as critic Douglas Murphy writes circa 2014:

An unpleasant sense of *déjà vu* occurs every time HRH The Prince of Wales comes down from Balmoral to pipe up about contemporary architecture. For more than 30 years now, he's been the bane of the architectural profession, wielding his accidental power to influence the design not only of individual buildings and projects, but the entire debate about what architecture is, who it is for and what it should look like.[3]

And then:

By the time Charles was making his pleas for traditional design based upon "timeless" principles, the dismantling of the welfare consensus of the postwar world was in full swing. Rejecting modern architecture went hand-in-hand with fighting the unions, deregulating the planned economy, smashing industry and rejecting the spectre of socialism that had almost ruined Britain.[4]

Huzzah for non-reform!

Murphy's intervention is worth exploring. He takes Charles's "ten key principles" for architecture and counters with ten of his own, both worth quoting in full:

Charles's Ten Key Principles . . .

- Developments must respect the land.
- Architecture is a language.
- Scale is also key.
- Harmony: neighboring buildings "in tune" but not uniform.
- The creation of well-designed enclosures.
- Materials also matter: local wood beats imported aluminum.
- Limit signage.
- Put the pedestrian at the center of the design process.
- Space is at a premium—but no high-rises.
- Build flexibility in.

. . . and Douglas Murphy's:

- **The city belongs to everyone**

Public space gets ever more murkily private; we need to redress the balance of who owns what. It's people like the prince that stand to lose out.

- **Your home is not a castle**

We'd be a far more equal and civilized island if the desire for home ownership wasn't pandered to at every turn.

- **Architecture is not a language**

The idea of an underlying grammar to architecture implies urban life peaked in the piazzas of Renaissance Florence—a period of pestilence, gangster princes, and public executions.

- **But architecture can still be read**

Buildings have no language. But the mightiest palace and the tiniest shed can tell us how those who build see the world and their place in it.

- **Mimesis is not mimicry**

Talented architects can work with classical traditions in contemporary architecture. It's unlikely Charles would recognize this if he saw it.

- **Honesty is still a virtue**

The architectural era Charles helped usher in was filled with inane jokes and frivolous nonsense. Architecture doesn't need to be fun.

- **The street isn't everything**

It's right that the importance of the street is recognized, but we must avoid turning city centers into identical forests of privatized space.

- **Nature is not our friend**

On respecting nature, let us quote Werner Herzog: "There is a harmony [to nature]—it is the harmony of overwhelming and collective murder."

- **Harmony involves dissonance**

Cities must improve their interactions with the natural world. This does not mean architecture must copy natural forms; rather it must reconcile itself with cycles of energy and material.

Change Is Coming

The next century will be pivotal for humanity, and architecture will play a huge role. Cute cottages with nice local stonework won't help.

This kind of controversy is familiar territory, alas, when those with influence weigh in on aesthetic issues. But the prince's "accidental power" must now be laid alongside the real power of an elected, even if in fact mandate-free, politician. Thus, worse because it might actually prove effective in law and practice, there is the American Trump Administration's 2020 call, "Making Federal Buildings Beautiful Again," for all national administrative buildings to be executed in classical Greek and Roman style. This directive is familiar confection of bogus populism and aesthetic retrenchment in favor of "beauty,"[5] if not cute cottages with nice local stonework.

Of course Ayn Rand's choice of architecture as a site for her Objectivist philosophy of individual independence and capitalist freedom is, in retrospect, somewhat bizarre. Architecture is the most collective of the applied arts, an undertaking impossible without the cooperation of many professionals beyond designer or designers, including HVAC and wiring experts, structural engineers, and construction companies. Moreover, any building requires a client, a developer, a municipally approved site, and zoning permissions.

More widely still, no building takes its place in the abstract isolation sometimes suggested by drawing or maquette. A building speaks to and is spoken to by its surrounds. Even beyond aesthetics, a building is a place within a city, a gathering of citizens who must work and walk around the creation. One may choose to visit an art gallery or not, and to view a given painting or sculpture within. One has no choice but to experience the architecture of the city.

And once more beyond that, a building, like any human creation, takes its place within both markets and environments, some financial and some natural. We cannot understand architecture without taking account of this widening gyre of influence and, sometimes, compromise. The designer and his or her design are just the beginning. The solitary genius, the "starchitect" of recent cultural celebrity, is kind of retroactive fiction, protagonist of a false narrative that can succeed only in distracting us from the realities of genuine building.

All of this is by way of noting something hollow about Rand's depiction of Roark as the "moral" architect, one single-mindedly dedicated to his singular vision against all obstacles. Rand commits both a conceptual and a political error, and allows her own ideological blindness to occlude the nuance of a profession whose genuine ethical demands are far more complex, and rewarding.

Wynand, meanwhile, is revealed as the slave of his own ambition, in apt urban metaphors: He "walked at random. He owned nothing but he was owned by any part of the city. It was right that the city should not direct his way and that he should be moved by the pull of chance corners. Here I am, my masters, I am coming to salute you and acknowledge, wherever you want me, I shall go as I am told. I'm the man who wanted power."

A moral ideal—who could argue with that? And then unwavering character and integrity over fashion and popular taste? Yes! It's easy to see how this stand-up morality would fetch the soul of an adolescent, the same way Holden Caulfield's complaints about "phoneyness" resonate with the person in search of genuineness in a world full of poseurs and fakes, and a life lived without fear or favor. Would that we could all exist with a guiding ideal that allowed us never to care what anyone else thinks. But the real ethical world is more complicated than that, for better and worse. It is of course bogus to worry too much about how we are seen by others—mostly they don't care, in fact—but it is essential to acknowledge that our actions and character have consequences on the world and the other people in it. There are no isolated heroes, and chance corners have their place in the ethical universe of the city. These are the lessons of architecture, not that solitary and totalizing aesthetic vision is the lodestar of moral life.

* * *

One way to conceive of the baseline issue here is to invoke a more traditional philosophical distinction, that between *Moralität* and *Sittlichkeit*. The former term, translatable simply as *morality*, is typically associated with individual assessment of one's actions in the world. Am I doing right or wrong, good or evil? In an influential iteration, Kant's categorical imperative involves the positive thought-experiment of asking whether the maxim governing a prospective action can be universalized as part of the moral law. This armchair abstract philosophizing is countered by Hegel's notion of organic fieldwork in ethical life, the site where *sittlich* relations are enacted in rich everydayness.

Hegel was of course no slouch at armchair abstraction too, but here he seems to be on the correct side. To use an additional insight drawn from the Western philosophical tradition, Aristotle argues that ethics speak to character, not just individual actions or decisions. The relation between character and action is dynamic: one reinforces the other over time, the life span of the potentially virtuous *phronimos*, or person of practical wisdom. No single action determines one's ethical status, but all actions are part of what makes up one's character.

Distinguishing ethics from morality is of course tricky, and sometimes there is semantic slippage that makes the effort begin to seem pointless, or comical. There is an excruciating scene in the 1999 comedy *Election* (d. Alexander Payne), where the hapless high school teacher Mr. M, played by Matthew Broderick, is about to become entangled in the overpowering ambition of office-seeking

Tracy Flick (Reese Witherspoon). Mr. M epically fails in his effort to get students to articulate the distinction between ethics and morals, though Tracy seems to have a pretty good grasp of it.

The film itself, as some critics have noted, is an essay in the distinction, especially as it applies to politics both electoral and personal. Do you want to do what you personally consider moral, or do you want to take part in a larger collective undertaking with enduring substance of social adhesion and virtue? Ethical life is that collective undertaking, the shared task of (as Aristotle put it) "living and faring well." If we want to understand the ethics of architecture, then, we cannot do so from the study. We must walk in the neighborhoods and cities where architecture happens.

To be sure, there will remain slippages between the concepts of morality and ethics. There are not reliably distinct as concepts. But we can trace some linguistic clues that may aid the investigation. People often refer to their personal ethics, perhaps less often to their personal morality. They mean, presumably, something more like Aristotelian character than an abstract rationalism on the Kantian model: ethics belong to them, while morality is a system or procedural. But nearby lies the murky secondary territory of *personal values* or, worse, *core values*—about which we mostly hear when some athlete, or corporation, or athletic corporation, apologizes for a given action that "does not reflect my/our core values."

Aristotle and others might beg to differ at this point: if you performed the action, then it belongs to your ethical life, and hence is part of your character. Perhaps the real meaning here is that such actions, in the apologist's eyes, fail to live up to their ethical *aspirations*—but that is a very different kettle of apologies, and values, whatever they are, are rendered pretty much irrelevant when we are talking about weakness of the will, ethical failure, studied blindness to wrongdoing, and bad decisions made in the heat of the moment.

Philosophers can, and will, debate these matters endlessly. More reliable, for our present purposes, is something like what the phrase *professional ethics* captures. Are there obligations that attend to a person *simply because* she or her is engaged in a certain kind of work, indeed are a function of that work? Here there may be a divide and even a conflict between purely personal obligation, or inclination, and what a professional identity demands.

Professions from medicine to law to (sometimes) journalism have adopted specific codes of ethics meant to capture these work-based obligations. Architecture is many things—art, craft, vocation, mere job—but it is surely a profession in this sense. This fact will be the backbone of everything that follows. What are the professional obligations of architects? But, as we will discover, this is no easily codifiable question.[6]

In the six succeeding chapters of this book, which might be better conceived as *memos* or *non-lectures* after the manner of Italo Calvino and E. E. Cummings, I propose to offer a kind of phenomenological tour of the ethical terrain on which architecture is built. It is a perambulation, but one with a purpose. And so there is another resonance now audible: Umberto Eco's six walks in the fictional woods. Numerologists and other occult experts may ponder why all of Calvino, Cummings, and Eco choose six as their magic number. One source suggests the following: "Number 6 is a symbol of deep emotions and compassion. . . . [Y]ou are a very caring person. You give love to others and others give love back to you. For you most important is to live your life in love and harmony."

That sounds bogus to me, but I'm not going to argue with other sixes: days of creation, hexagrams, tumbling dice, and maybe lurking devilishness. Fine, go crazy with boxcars. But thinking of dice always takes me back to those old *Dungeons & Dragons* days, when we used twelve-sided dice—dodecahedrons in math-speak, and also one of the Platonic celestial solids if you're into that—to determine our moment-to-moment fates. Two sixes are better than one, in craps or D&D, but I will stick to one in what follows. The walks are long or short depending on topic, and they are maybe, if I can help myself to one more inspirational figure working on a level far above this one, sometimes executed in the spirit of Walter Benjamin's strolls through the arcades of Paris. We look, we reflect, we philosophize.

I didn't end up going to architecture school, probably for better rather than worse, but architecture has been a personal and professional interest of mine for many years now. The people responsible for this are detailed elsewhere in this volume, but as we start out on our six walks, let me simply acknowledge the fifteen-year-old version of myself, gone for four decades and more, who made me think that creating objects in the world is one of the noblest and most difficult things humans have chosen to do. Ethical life is many things, but none is more essential than building.

A colleague of mine, a distinguished writer and architect, told me not long ago that when he was in architecture school, there were no dedicated ethics classes.[7] They simply did not exist. Of course, there are now such classes at many leading institutions, often on the model of medical or legal training. But my colleague had one instructor who started every class by asking, "Who do you work for?" It is an excellent question; in fact it is always the central question.

Do you work for the clients? Sure, they're the ones paying you. But do you also work for the community? The profession? The standards of aesthetics and design excellence within the craft? Social justice in an ever-larger political context? How about accessibility concerns in a world where the human and nonhuman forms are ever evolving? Do you maybe execute for something even more exalted than from, such as—without being pretentious—Being or Life?

One of my favorite texts about architecture is a list called "Two Hundred and Fifty Things an Architect Should Know," composed by the architect and urbanist Michael Sorkin, who died just a few days before I wrote this sentence.[8] The desirable knowledge listed by Sorkin ranges from "the feel of cool marble under bare feet" to "the Gini coefficient" and "the proper proportions of a gin martini." Architectural failures are mentioned, as are Aristotle, Friedrich Engels, Walter Benjamin, and Guy Debord. "*Stadtluft macht frei*" makes an appearance at 210, "Dawn breaking after a bender" at 181—cross-reference that with gin martini, perhaps, not to mention "Good Bordeaux" (128) and "Good beer" (129). But my personal favorites are "How to get lost" (96), "The need for freaks" (82), and then an essential sequence relevant to our being here together right now: "What the client wants" (39), "What the client thinks it wants" (40), "What the client can afford" (41), "What the planet can afford" (42).

Who do you work for? That seemingly simple but actually very difficult question is what this short book is about. Let's start walking—and maybe get lost.

1

Creating Buildings

In 1923, Charles-Édouard Jeanneret, known better by his self-applied professional name Le Corbusier, published what would eventually be hailed as the most influential book of architectural theory since Vitruvius. Le Corbusier's *Vers une architecture* (in English, rendered as either *Towards a Modern Architecture* or *Toward an Architecture*)[1] was less a technical primer about built forms than it was an aesthetic manifesto and, after its fashion, a quirky *ars poetica*: an architectural primer on how to write architectural primers. The very idea of design is uniquely queried and explored. The forms of tall residential buildings and city plans that would later be recognized as typically Corbusian are present; but so are appreciations of everyday objects, including automobiles, household objects, and airplanes.

The basic rhetorical direction of Le Corbusier's book is straightforward, and shared with other Modernist aesthetic movements: the new century requires clean lines and beautiful revelation of functionality. Designers should abandon decoration and bogus classicism. Indeed, the book began as an extension of Adolf Loos's famous argument in "Ornament and Crime" (1910–1913) that "No ornament can any longer be made today by anyone who lives on our cultural level . . . Freedom from ornament is a sign of spiritual strength." Both Loos and Le Corbusier stopped short of the nihilistic speed-fetishism of Filippo Tommaso Marinetti, whose own Futurist manifesto of creative destruction first appeared in 1909, but there is a shared demand, here, for fresh air and clean features. In the work of a Futurist architect such as Antonio Sant'Elia one can discern forms that Le Corbusier might have approved. And yet, Marinetti was a fascist, aligning his passion with Mussolini, while Le Corbusier

The Ethics of Architecture. Mark Kingwell, Oxford University Press (2021). © Mark Kingwell.
DOI: 10.1093/oso/9780197558546.003.0002

emerges as the great scion of democratized living. Le Corbusier's 1929 "City of Tomorrow" proposal, published in sketches but never built, is a brilliant imagining of how comfort and harmony might be achieved on a large urban scale. These are the differing modes of Modernism: destroy to create, or create to enable. As always, the stakes are political as well as aesthetic. Indeed, there can be no separation between them.

In this walk or non-lecture, I will dilate a little on and challenge the relationship between aesthetics and politics in the realm of architecture and urban design. My aim is an analytic but passionate engagement with the idea of public justice, as realized (or mostly not) in the built environment. Vitruvius had maintained that the key components of all good architecture were *firmitas, utilitas, venustas,* usually rendered in English as "commodity, firmness, and delight." These admirable aesthetic goals may not seem to possess obvious ethical or political valence, but in the proposed work I am going to draw out the specifically justice-based significance of design, especially in large conurbations that currently host most of the planet's population.

It is no longer viable, if indeed it ever was, to design a building or plan a city with regard for isolated aesthetic ends. Architecture is the most public, and most unavoidable, version of the applied arts, and its undertaking is a form of social trust. The current project builds on my previous work in contextualizing a single building[2] and in exploring how cities shape experience.[3] It will also draw on my recent reflections concerning technological immersion, the relation between concrete and virtual, and the changing status of "the human" as technology advances from primitive Artificial Intelligence (AI) to algorithms and systems closer to sentience, consciousness, and possibly self-direction—generalized autonomous intelligence artifices, or GAIAs. This will involve consideration of, among other things, The Singularity: that is, the so far notional point at which nonhuman algorithmic robustness surpasses the human version and becomes potentially self-generating and evolutionary.[4] On this technological terrain, so-called smart buildings are just the beginning; the end might be the transformation of architectural practice, and perhaps even the end of human-designed architecture itself.[5]

The phrase "city of tomorrow" has a utopian ring to it, and it is certainly true that utopian schemes have long been favored by urban designers, from Thomas More's original sixteenth-century Utopia to the mid-twentieth-century German "Stadt von Morgen" to the Radiant City, Milton Keynes, and Levittown suburban dreams of postwar city planners. For every utopia there has been, naturally, an equal and opposite dystopian realization: the dead-end concrete byways of British towns, the high-rise slums of American and Canadian cities, or perhaps just the banal and enervating monster-home sub-developments of exurban sprawl. At least since Plato sketched his just city in the *Republic*—the city of tomorrow realized today, if we just eliminate the older people!—critics have worried that large-scale schemes are inherently unjust, sometimes to exactly the extent that they pursue justice. But abandoning the idea that cities should be sites of a just and equitable political order is too hasty, and perhaps calamitous.

Why? Because *all* cities are cities of tomorrow, since they are guided by the desires of their inhabitants; and so our current cluster of urban issues, which could look as though restricted to zoning or mixing of use or dubious public-private capital ventures, are too pressing to leave undertheorized. There are ethical and political dimensions in every plan or development. Can we afford to build more beachside condominiums in Miami? Are smart systems of traffic control and shopping maps really working to aid us? In this series of reflective non-lectures we deploy not so much utopian as *anti-anti-utopian* energy. We will ask: What responsibility do designers and builders hold in respect of their work? The aim is to render a compact but comprehensive account of the ethical and political obligations of architects. Buildings create the environments in which most humans work, relate, play, and pursue their desires. They change the contours of the unbuilt environment in which they are erected. They create vistas and declivities that sculpt the earth on which we walk. And they perform—or fail to—a list of crucial functions that are primordial to human existence: shelter, sustenance, social relations, political possibility, and aesthetic exaltation.

There is a surprising dearth of rigorous reflection on the politics of such a potent dimension of the human project. War, money, identity, health, and abstract interpersonal relations of blame and responsibility have received vastly more attention in the literature of ethical reflection—even as the purveyors of these discourses have perforce eaten, slept, met, and argued in buildings. This casual occlusion of the material conditions of our lifeworld, the disappearing non-reality of what makes "reality" possible, is the background concern of this project. I envision a study that is part analysis and part manifesto—or maybe all that plus a *cri de coeur*. Architecture can be evil or it can be virtuous. We must not let it be either without a serious theoretical challenge.[6]

Let us begin with specific aspects of the architect's responsibilities. Some of these are obvious: to build well and truly, with competence and professional dedication; to honor obligations to clients and coworkers; to acknowledge errors and defects with honest humility. These are no different from the obligations of any professional—though, in common with the engineer or pilot (say), in this case errors of professional judgment may involve human costs unknown to the failures of the errant humanist or social scientist.

Beyond these, though, lurk the complicated obligations of aesthetic style and influence. For many if not most architects, this is boggy ground. "Style" is sometimes considered a tainted word in the common discourse of the profession, and yet it is an essential element not just of the individual practice of a firm or singular designer, but also of the larger trends that govern the development of any art form, including one that is at the same moment practical, applied, efficient, and functional. Style encompasses a host of political choices, not just aesthetic ones.

Upstream of all of this runs a civic obligation that some architects and planners have been reluctant to acknowledge. I mean the civic or communal aspects of what they do, in particular the environmental ones. The matter is not simply one of how a given building relates to its surrounding context, or even the very specific issues of whether a structure is coded for defensible use or meets standards of LEED certification or affordable housing. It is a deeper question of whether the designer is, or should be, an agent of social betterment in his or her work, an artist whose engagements with the world might aspire to make that world better. Or is this the work of users and citizens? So-called smart buildings and neighborhoods, perhaps eventually entire cities, may aid us in realizing goals of convenience, but only at the cost of perpetual surveillance, data-gathering, and technological domination.

Finally, there is an even more controversial arena of architectural reflection, significantly influenced by Heidegger and his followers, concerning the ontological significance of architecture. Are buildings necessarily sites, as Heidegger suggested, of fundamental existential reflection? How might this be an issue of justice? Well, we know that some buildings are holy: temples and churches, long houses and pagodas. But architecture can also be boring, or banal, or actively punishing in the form of its aid to carceral states (the torture chamber, the panopticon) and bureaucratic immiseration (the windowless office, the cube farm). Here we confront ethical and political problems hosted by design itself.[7]

We have always been shaped by our buildings and neighborhoods, even as we shaped them. We are now hybrid creatures, transhuman cyborg selves, whose notion of humanity is decisively fused with enveloping technology. Is this the city of tomorrow—assuming we are even able to make it to tomorrow?

Our urban surroundings cannot help but reflect the kind of society we live in, and affect profoundly the mental architecture of our consciousness as citizens. The agora of Athens certainly was more than just a place to stroll about and make observations about the weather. The magnificent broad avenues of many European cities represent more than simply grandeur and civic optimism—they also made it easier for mounted cavalry to rout a disobedient mass of citizens. And the kind of urban world we build for ourselves today will determine whether we have the civic vocabulary to be more than just a society of consumers—whether we have room amidst our shopping malls and expressways to squeeze in the occasional agora.

* * *

In what follows in this first non-lecture, I raise some issues concerning the political implications of the built environment, in particular the way structures of civic and domestic space interact to influence the character of individuals as citizens. These remarks began life as an intervention concerning the ethics of a particular profession, architecture, under conditions of globalization; but soon the lines of argument took a turn—natural-seeming, to me anyway—away from the rather limited concerns of professional conduct, indeed away from ethical theory in the narrow sense, into a more contextual and activist direction.[8]

The issues of appropriate professional practice quickly acquire, to my mind, a crucial political dimension. In a sense, therefore, the following is merely an extended illustration of the Aristotelian dictum (minus the Aristotelian naturalism and certainty) that ethics and politics are intimately related subjects, both concerned with how to live well together, how to flourish as humans—and that such a project always includes, centrally, issues of place making.

My first claim, perhaps an obvious one, is that the current need for a globalized politics to counteract the already dominant globalized market and globalized culture—a global politics that does not simply collapse down to a spastic form of neoliberal orthodoxy—can be aided by the responsible practice of architecture. It follows that this renewed form of cosmopolitanism can, equally, be harmed by the absence of such a practice. I say this boldly here, but want at the same time to be mindful of the limitations of such a claim. Architects are by no means the only individuals, or professionals, whose actions have a central role in any renewed sense of transnational citizenship. They are bound by conditions of possibility as restrictive as anything encountered in other walks of life, hampered by building codes and financing difficulties, working with and around client desires, and so on. Many face a daily grind of poring over construction codes or preparing drawings for projects they dislike. They have personal responsibilities that are not political, and there are other political players besides themselves on the field.

Nevertheless, my second, perhaps less obvious, claim is that architects, insofar as they control the means of shaping the spaces of everyday life, must put themselves in the vanguard of the new global citizenship. I use the word "control" without, I hope, overestimating their ability to influence a given project from start to finish. This ability may be quite limited; and without wanting to suggest an elevated, arrogant magisterial role for the architect, there is a dangerous self-image of the artist-genius who imposes his vision on the aesthetically impoverished mundane realm, from the fictional hauteur of Howard Roark to the real-world *avant-garde* conceits of Rem Koolhaas, Daniel Liebeskind, or Peter Eisenman.[9]

But because the built environment is so inescapable for all of us, and because we so often feel alienated from that environment—when it should be a site of our aspiration, our discourse about who we are or might be—architects have a deeper political role than is sometimes recognized. Builders must make it possible for dwellers to act. In the highly charged political atmosphere of our speedy times, it is not enough to conceive ethical obligations as confined to meeting clients' needs, or even to staying true to a certain vision of professional integrity. Shapers of space need to reconceive their task as uncovering the utopian and revolutionary possibilities of building, of opening up spaces for political thought and action.

In choosing to speak of building, dwelling, and acting, I of course allude to Heidegger's celebrated essay "Building Dwelling Thinking," and the argument there that dwelling is the essence of mortal human life.[10] In *dwelling*, rather than merely inhabiting or existing, we are so situated in the world that we can *think*, can reflect the conditions of our own existence, and take insight from that reflection. Contemplation of what Heidegger calls *the fourfold*—earth, sky, mortals, gods—is therefore implied in the practice of building, since that is what creates the possibility of being situated reflectively, so that we can tarry in thought. A bridge, for example, gathers the landscape around it into a structure of thought, producing that specifically meaningful place, a location. The force of this argument remains undiminished: we build in order to dwell, indeed can build only when dwelling is the goal.

But, to put it rather crudely, this is not the time for us to tarry too long, or too exclusively, in thoughts of the fourfold. This is a time to act as well as to think. Or, perhaps more accurately, it is a time to act in order that thought should (once more?) become possible: to uncover an activist, discursive politics that is, as I shall put it, grimly utopian. For it is characteristic of the current waves of market-driven development that they are murderous of thought, sometimes most thoroughly so when they are most outwardly successful: when they reinforce the widespread tendency to accept clearly harmful trends as inevitable if they are backed by enough fast-flowing capital. I think here, for example, of the unreflective and empty modernism of the massive Potsdamer Platz reconstruction; or of the huge chunks of land swallowed every year by exurban sprawl, a process of "development" successful only in the twinned sense of offering financial return on highly concentrated investment and taking land away from the environment.[11]

Before we surrender to a bland future of zombie-like privatization and consumerism, disappearing into a maze of freeways and shopping malls, slab-like downtowns and gated communities, we need to act to make thought, not just the already thought, a part of our political discourse. Let us ask, as builders and dwellers both, what we can do to make this a world we want, not just a world that happens to us.

I think we can best approach this complicated project by opening up the larger question of what globalization of culture and money is doing to us as individuals, by attempting to influence some small chunk of our world through our choices. We tend to think of the problems of globalization and cultural identity, and their complicated relation to the built environment, as peculiar to our times. But in fact they are rooted in ancient ideas of civic belonging, the need to create and maintain social spaces: rooted in the twenty-six acres of the Athenian agora, the enclosed courts of the medieval universities, the glowing arcades of the nineteenth century. And the politico-cultural crisis we now face is at least as old as the century that has just ended, if not older. It is, in its way, a crisis of modernity itself, and has to do with the complex, isomorphic relationship between individuals and the social and cultural fields that surround them: a troubled relationship of inside and outside, and of the various boundaries that mark and move between these discrete spaces.

Both cultures and individuals are subject to the pluralistic conditions typical of late modernity. Indeed, a feasible general characterization of modernity is naturally that of a program of deliberate breaks from tradition or inherited stability. Ezra Pound's celebrated imperative, "Make it new," is only the most succinct expression of this desire, so peculiar and so powerful in the twentieth century. This freedom from the past has, notoriously, both costs and benefits. Definitions and singleness are thrown over in favor of fluidity and provisionality, but this is a toss that unsettles as much as it liberates. We are forever in danger of losing perspective in a relentless demand for speedy novelty, coupled with its unlikely twin, the been-there, done-that insouciance of the jaded aesthete—or, nowadays, the bored consumer.

Consider: when Proust says of his character Albertine, in *A la Recherche du temps perdu*, that she "is no longer a woman, but a series of events," he expresses something crucial about the dawning sensibility of the new century, a dawning precariously dated by Virginia Woolf as occurring in December 1910, when an episode of drawing-room frankness about casual sex convinced her that traditional morality was over. Joyce's Bloom, walking through the crowded landscape of a single day's consciousness, maps the same terrain, and gives some sense of modern art's struggles to slow down, in imperfect media like language or pigment, the quickness that is the new century's soul.

Proust proposes attaching to Albertine "a sign corresponding to what in physics is the sign that indicates velocity." She is no longer a person, as that notion was once understood by moralists and philosophers; she is now, instead, as the critic Peter Conrad nicely puts it, a vector, a trace of speed in a continuum of indeterminacies as complex as anything sketched by the special theory of relativity. She is, too, the fractured face of cubism, or the meaning-making soul on overdrive, fashioning more language and imagery than it can understand, as diagnosed by Freud. She is modern. The world no longer means what it did, and the people within it, if they are able to shore up their fragments against the wrack of change, are no longer the same creatures as their premodern forebears. Character, in the sense of the well-formed disposition to act with integrity—a word whose etymology invokes the oneness of the integer—gives way to a layered and shifting selfhood, the "multiple subject positions" of more recent fashionable theory. And speed becomes the dominant trope of self-expression and self-regard.

This shift is real and its consequences but poorly understood even now, ten decades on. At its banal end, it makes for individuals who are reduced to clusters of spending patterns or retail choices— the annihilation of self in the steady, dead-eyed gaze of the brand-experiential demographer or corporate-financed cool-hunter. These are the anthropologists of the new global market, who no longer perceive persons with stories to tell but only pathways traced from door to product; no longer see individuals but only half-formed nodes in the culture/cash nexus. Even in a more reflective part of the spectrum, plurality is likewise endemic, retaining its unsettling force in the demands of multiple conflicting values or norms: duty to country over duty to self; the value of loyalty as against the value of honesty; family tradition over individual ambition.

These deeper conflicts, while not unknown to the premodern mind, nevertheless attain a greater force when the project of personal self-fulfillment, abetted by the democratization of leisure and art, begins to vie in importance with more traditional social roles. It is only in a modern world where everyone is expected to be the artist of his or her own life, in other words, that some of the deep conflicts of our experience become possible. It is only when we are constantly told that we must create a unified identity that we see just how fractured our identities really are. As ever, modernity generates its own self-destructive crisis.

Often such conflicts are characterized as battles between self and culture, as if one were constantly attempting to shake off the bonds of expectation, perhaps in the manner of that powerful late twentieth-century creation, the teenager. But to what extent is culture itself reworked and relativized here, made a fetish-object or cheap form of aide-memoire? Once more, we tend to think of the banalization of culture as a recent blight, what with our multiethnic celebrations of food and clothing or our commodification of foreignness via tourism; but the evidence indicates a longer timeline. Indeed, it suggests that cultures begin to lose their integrity at just the same time individuals do.

The Viennese satirist Karl Kraus captured the problem with characteristic economy in the early part of the twentieth century. Among other virtues, Kraus was responsible for labeling the proto-Nazi camp-followers of Oswald Spengler's *The Decline of the West*—in German, *Der Untergang des Abendlandes*—the "untergangsters." He dubbed the Austro-Hungarian Empire "Kakania" in a scatological play on Emperor Franz Josef's ubiquitous *K. und K.* (kaiser and king) symbolism and seal.

As the critic Peter Conrad writes: "In Kraus's view Kakania gave the rest of the continent a lesson in falsity. Europe, he thought, had become a cheap and nasty variety shop. The states that emerged from that world-ending war covered up their political duplicity and economic distress by selling tawdry souvenirs to tourists—the *papier-mâché* helmets of London policemen, dwarfed Eiffel Towers, perhaps (for connoisseurs) a silver rose in plastic. . . . Culture was merely a costume party, and the purpose of travel is to try on funny hats."[12] Television's Homer Simpson, characteristically, makes the point with more economy. Seeing an Indian film on his own TV, he crows, "They wear different clothes than we do! That's funny!"

On both sides of the individual/cultural divide, then, the effects of the revolution in sensibility are palpable, and not always positive. Variety can lead to the tyranny of choice. Fluidity can be another word for confusion. It is therefore no surprise, I think, that the story of modernity is one of simultaneous promise and ennui, the bipolar disorder of aspiration and boredom. For every enthusiast like the Futurist Marinetti, who saw swift machines releasing us from our servitude to the vile earth, there is a countervailing languid Wildean aesthete or *weltschmerzlich* Schopenhauerian nihilist, who finds superiority instead in a boredom with everything new or fast—a boredom, which, to be sure, is constantly renewed under the false sign of its relief via stimulation.[13]

The postmodern cool of a figure like Koolhaas—as persona, if not necessarily as designer—might be considered a contemporary fusion of these two attitudes. He is at once drawn to innovation and technology but pretends a disdain for everything meaningful or ordered. He celebrates "the city as unauthorized event" even as urban landscapes sprawl out of control and concentrate wealth and power in tiny nodes. Such a combination is inherently unstable. For every cultural innovation that promises a more fulfilling and liberating sense of personal identity, there is a mass-produced hat or parodied dance craze that makes cultural belonging an empty gesture, akin to joining a hobby club or reading the books that were once upon a time recommended by Oprah Winfrey. Nowadays the former global TV star spends most of her energy on Twitter. Of course she does.

In the field of intellectual life, meanwhile, far too much contemporary theorizing simply has not helped us get a grasp on the rich dilemmas of our particularity. For every open field of possibility, which seems to offer a glimpse of ourselves as freely created artworks in progress, there is now a corresponding form of reductionism: materialist accounts of emotion, demographic accounts of reason, psychotherapeutic accounts of motivation. These rob us of agency and whirl us back into an ethically and politically vacuous world of random mutations, spinning atoms, and unquantifiable risks. Multiple subject identities are not proof against concentrated wealth or rearguard essentialism.

Under these conditions cultural defense ultimately becomes a kind of fetishism, and identity declines into nothing more than the timeworn chauvinism of excluding the out-groupers. Excessive regard for national sovereignty, meanwhile, just means now that our hands are tied when it comes to passing judgment on, say, the systemic murder of Kosovars in the Balkans, labeling it a civil war and engaging in an extended moral debate that contrives to leave everything very much as it is. For every apparent gain, in short, we now forcibly observe a balancing danger. This is the modern (and sometimes postmodern or even post-postmodern) world.

* * *

For these reasons among others, then, we cannot address the political emptiness of our de facto global culture by simply continuing the talk about nations and their laws; or by allowing local debate to continue as if political choices were not conditioned by, and implicated in, complex events around the swiftly shrinking, indeed almost non-spatial, globe. Such moves simply surrender the larger field to the power of corporations and high-speed capital to create and dominate markets, to rape the environment, and to amass profit without regard for the labor that actually generates wealth.

So much is clear. What is not clear to many people is what, precisely, we can do about it. The task of any useful theory of citizenship is therefore to provide a sense of meaningful political activity in a world where such activity is ever threatened with meaninglessness. We have to press the internal commitments of globalism rather than retreat from it. We have to make the new cosmopolitan ideal not just a marketer's dream, an image from a Benetton ad campaign, but a political reality.

We must, furthermore, create a new, and newly complex, sense of belonging that embraces differences as well as transcends them, that forges commitment across boundaries without erasing the things that make those boundaries interesting in the first place. The public spaces we inhabit are a crucial site of this creation. Already it is impossible to travel the world without coming across a Disney store or a McDonald's or a Nine West outlet in some public square. We could hardly count it a victory if we simply reproduced that deadening sameness at the level of the citizenry.

As Walter Benjamin's extended engagements with the world of things remind us, constructing a stable identity in the dreamscape of the Arcades—or the dreamscape of the shopping mall and Internet—is a project fraught with overdetermination. There are always, as my ultracool post-cultural students well know, too many options, too many choices.[14] Paradoxically, the problems of politics often arise today not in the form of a problem of scarcity, but as one of abundance. We have too much, too many things to choose from, and that effectively distracts us from forming the concrete intentions to address the more basic issue of uneven distribution of things and choices.

We are so intent on dealing with our own condition of having too much information and too many brands—this is a genuine challenge, as we all know in the high-speed First World—that we often miss those who have too little, too few. A surfeit of options may be considered both a blessing and a curse, of course. One's attitude to the volume and velocity of everyday life can vary from day to day, and it often depends simply on how fast you like to go, how much of a multitasker you want to be. And yet there is one sense in which we have no option. Politically, we cannot begin elsewhere than with the surfeited social-cultural environment that already shapes us.

That sentiment may sound defeatist, given that it begins from something that many people find overwhelming. And in some critics' hands it might be another and more sophisticated form of the same complacency that seems to come over cheerleaders of globalization whenever they put pen to paper. But I am suggesting something far more radical. Here we have to follow Benjamin—not to mention Plato—in tacking along the line where hope meets despair.[15] Without losing the thoroughgoing mindfulness of our own limitations (in foresight and goodwill, in time and energy), we can perhaps begin to articulate a sort of realistic wishfulness, a worldly utopianism.

An action-oriented conception of citizenship is, first and foremost, engaged with other people in the creation of shared social spaces and in the discourse that such spaces make possible. Through participation and conversation, we reproduce our social meanings through time: that is what culture is. Squares and institutions, walkways and stadiums, these are the places where the dreams of a people are realized in stone and iron, glass and air. They are sites of politics, not merely of design or style; or rather, here design and style are themselves aspects of the larger political imaginaries.

By the same token, when those spaces are taken away from us, violently or by stealth, we are diminished in ourselves and in our politics. Benjamin, visiting Moscow in 1926, was disturbed by the starkness of the public space, so conditioned by revolutionary ideas. "There are no cafés. Impossible to get a drink," he wrote. "Free trade and free intellect have been abolished. The cafes are therefore deprived of their public." There were no flâneurs, no idleness, no urban contingency, no fun. With their communal rooms, shared childrearing, and workers' clubs where leisure was cooperative and regimented, the Soviets had allocated fifteen square meters of space to each citizen—and along the way found "a radical means of expelling 'cosiness,'" and the cloying sentimentality of bourgeois individualism.

Benjamin was ambivalent about coziness—the prized bourgeois-interior quality of *Gemütlichkeit*—but we can still hear in his urbanite's complaint the longing for genuine public space. Revolution has swept away the nooks and crannies, leaving only the vast open squares of triumph. Vladimir Mayakovsky had written of the 1919 revolution that "the streets are our brushes, the squares our palettes," but the result was a canvas of unremitting seriousness. Le Corbusier, in Moscow at about the same time to design Centrosoyuz, the head office of the consumer cooperatives, noted that "The people take things seriously." It is part of the self-chosen task of political revolutions to reorder space and time, to mold them in the image of the new order: renaming the months, rewriting history, rebuilding the cities. Sometimes—in Tiananmen Square in 1989, say—a formerly glorious revolution is challenged by a new upheaval of political force on the very same ground that was set aside in celebration of the first, now moribund, act of emancipation.

I have used these examples from the revolutionary politics of the left, and that might seem to cut against the very idea of utopian political action. But my worldly utopianism is not revolutionary in that violent sense: I am not advocating the ruthless elimination of everything existing. It is also worth noting that the very same task of structuring social space is of course just as often—these days, much more often and more pervasively—undertaken by the forces of conservatism, usually with more money and slyness, less violence and noise. Benjamin's example of Baron Haussmann's boulevards in Paris, which tipped the balance away from harrying street fighters and toward mounted cavalry, is to the point. In my own city, there are still intricate cow gate entrances to certain public buildings, allegedly constructed to slow down storming protesters who might want to march on the lawmakers and have it out. Free-trade zones and exurban sprawl, even the 33 percent increase in domestic housing size, are all examples of a much more widespread and alienating distortion of the built environment than any leftist revolutionary could ever hope to effect.

All social space is suffused with political meanings and agendas, the very stones and walls a kind of testament to the ongoing struggles for liberation and justice. And as with space, so with time. We should never forget that the legal profession has managed what neither the Jacobin revolutionaries nor the scientific community could, namely to recast time on a functional base-ten model, measuring out advice and influence in six-minute tenths. Nor should we fail to notice that the eternal now of our speedy times is, functionally, a form of forgetting—a way of leaving the status quo mostly intact through the distracting power of constant novelty, and of equally constant nostalgia.

* * *

With these thoughts in mind, let us return to the issue of dwelling, and the building that makes it possible—and do so, now that I have mentioned domestic space explicitly, with some attention to the main site of our dwelling, the home. Home exerts a powerful effect in this field of thinking, and for more than the surface reasons. It is characteristic of the cultural effects I have been describing to make us think that we can get home by going more quickly forward or by retreating back. The crucial insight here is that neither course will really take us where we want to go, and meanwhile the home retreats more and more from the critical engagements necessary among disconnected global citizens.

Even recent attempts to reshape the home as a more open and public space—here I think of the Un-Private Houses of a 1999 Museum of Modern Art exhibition, about which I have written elsewhere—have the ultimate effect of simply making it more permeable to the anxieties of work.[16] In most cases, the project of the un-private houses is a matter of putting the self on view, of finding the presence of the imagined observer somehow reassuring. But that is not active engagement with the world outside; and it is not really a transcendence of privacy. It is merely an empty inwardness disguised as critique. Real progression in inhabitation involves something more than this new form of supremely elegant, but often banal narcissism; it involves the private realm influencing the public through a sustained critical engagement. This can be hard to see, especially if we are moved by the apparently liberating possibilities of our now-constant immersion in technology, the sort of transvaluation of traditional values celebrated by Donna Haraway in her 1985 essay, "Manifesto for Cyborgs."[17]

"The cyborg is resolutely committed to partiality, irony, intimacy, and perversity," Haraway writes. It is oppositional, utopian, and completely without innocence. No longer structured by the polarity of public and private, the cyborg defines a technological polis based partly on a revolution of social relations in the *oikos*, the household. Nature and culture are reworked; the one can no longer be the resource for the appropriation or incorporation by the other.

Yet we have been slow to accept the alteration of our natures through technology, a story which in truth is the story of human history but which tends, in practice, to become the story of the twentieth century. The reason for this truncation in scope is obvious enough, and is symbolized in a few choice inventions that, though in some cases born earlier, only come into their own during the bloody century: the machine gun, the airplane, the automobile, the telephone, the television, the computer. Mass production and mass destruction are the twinned pinnacles of twentieth-century life, and we still pledge our allegiance to them at every moment.

One consequence of this fact is the inescapability of capitalism—something that is sometimes challenged but mostly just accepted, indeed celebrated. Whether we like it or not, our bodies themselves now underwrite the dominance of the market, because every moment of waking and sleeping life is shot through with commitment to the goods and services of the global economy. We are capitalism made flesh. Another consequence is a profound change in our sense of ourselves, a change best caught by the somewhat misleading label "post-evolutionary." Our mastery of technology means we are no longer beholden to the gene pool. We can now shape and perpetuate it independently of natural reproduction, without all the attendant risks and tempestuous emotions. We are no longer bound by our natural environment, which we can also shape—though on the whole we seem bent on destroying it instead.

Of course, the limit of the natural environment is one reason the post-evolutionary label is misleading: we are still constrained at the baseline by natural facts, even if this baseline is always shifting because of our ingenuity and rapacity. The other reason to be suspicious of the label is that we are of course still evolving, if not quite in the manner of crude Darwinian orthodoxy.

What does all this entail in politics? First of all, an additional citizenly obligation, namely to attend to and understand the conditions of our technological existence—however painful that may be. This is primarily a matter of resisting the ideology of inevitability that creeps up around technology—an ideology so stealthy and complete, and so intimately related to the very idea of capital, that it is functionally invisible. But it is also a matter of plotting connections—connections that are often resisted or simply ignored as people surf on by—between machines and politics.

It is common these days for those of us in the privileged world to carry on large parts of our existence via e-mail, creating little virtual agoras out of our far-flung friends; or organizing dissent via the decentralized medium of the Internet. But these ethereal movements must nevertheless issue in the still-indispensable actions of shared space, if they are to be truly effective. The anti-corporatist protests of June 18 and November 30, 1999, or April 2000, for instance, and then subsequent Occupy protests of the later 2000s,[18] so effectively drawn from otherwise diffuse quarters, would have meant far less if they had not led to 40,000 people occupying the streets of Seattle, or 500 of them engaging in the highest form of citizenship, peaceful civil disobedience leading to arrest. (Sometimes, more intimately, a friendship blossoms in the strangely intimate space of e-mail. But it is complete only when we are together and my regard for you can register in the unequivocal, vulnerable, subtle media of the physical senses—when I can look into your eyes, see and touch your beautiful face, smell your personal perfume, just be next to you.)

In the face of rapidly changing technology, there is therefore a deeper obligation still, to reconceive not only citizenship and political commitment for a new era, but human nature itself. In 1928 Benjamin noted that technology is not best understood, as people often say, as the mastery of nature; it is, rather, the mastery of the relationship between nature and humankind. ("Men as a species completed their development thousands of years ago," he writes, "but humankind as a species is just beginning his.")[19] That is why Haraway and other Transhumanist prophets are only half right— or rather, more accurately, why we have only appreciated half, the unironic and apolitical half, of what they have been telling us.

Yes, we are all cyborgs now, mixed human-carbon hybrids with wires shooting through our watery bodies at every angle. But we have not yet managed the political implications of this fact, lost in the play of speed and pleasure that the wiring makes possible. We are too much taken with novelty and the "loveliness" of our inventions, the pure electromagnetic wave functions of next-generation technology. Technology becomes a sort of generalized deity, a wispy but all-pervasive god, especially in the form of the handheld smartphone, loaded with apps. Thus our great avoidance rituals in the face of technology, such that we fixate on the cutting edge and lose sight of the majority stuck on the trailing one. Or, if political issues do come up, the way we imagine they are about something like greater access to hardware—when they might really be about greater access to the human software of literacy, that indispensable enabling condition of citizenship, that forgotten civil right.

"Our best machines are made of sunshine," notes Haraway. That is both a virtue and a vice. Lightness and invisibility, the traits of the effective guerrilla, also entail, where power is entrenched, a lack of accountability. The genuine citizen-cyborg must send out as well as allow in; she must transmit as well as receive. There is no such thing as a one-way communications node. The difficulty with un-private houses and other projects of personal gratification, therefore, the difficulty with all these entertaining machines we keep giving ourselves, is not the old one of folding domesticity and privacy away from the public view, making that realm female and subordinate. It is rather that, in being so entirely permeable to the public view, privacy becomes merely an opportunity for conspicuous consumption.

This is the final subversion of the specter of the public as a means of resented surveillance, indeed rendering the very idea of surveillance meaningless by offering the world a complete view of everything that goes on in the house. But now the very idea of the polis as a shared space—a space shared for the purposes of discourse about how we may (or may not) all live together, not for the crude insistence on a single vision of the good life—is undermined in an ostentatious display of private enjoyment. The old public/private ideology is not transcended but simply reinscribed in a new, less obvious manner. Here political action is not so much prevented as nullified, made supremely uninteresting compared to the local pleasures of the house. Why should anyone bother with public spaces and the demanding actions of citizenship? Comfort becomes its own answer, shopping and surfing and e-trading their own defense.

This won't do. We need the separate private realm not only to escape the demanding pressures of public responsibility now and then, but also to engage more effectively with the shared, common aspects of life—to make us the sort of citizens who can actively create and maintain the essential third spaces of civil society when we do enter into them. Whatever its many dangers and shortcomings, a well-ordered private realm makes a just public realm possible. Among other things, it makes the public/private distinction itself a matter for specifically public discourse, a contested border war. For only there can we offer arguments that will be assessed by our fellow citizens—or those who might be. (As Haraway notes, the nature/culture, human/animal, and body/machine border wars are similarly demanding: there is "pleasure in the confusion of boundaries," she says, but also "responsibility in their construction.")

Importantly, we do not—cannot—any longer expect these conflicts to resolve themselves into some larger notional whole, some form of dialectical completeness or super-consensus that rises above our disagreements. Nor can we indulge the dangerous nostalgic vision of a perfect political harmony we have lost and must restore. Consensus is not really the goal of political discourse, which necessarily thrives on dissent; and nostalgia is just a comforting distraction we can ill afford. Instead of these vector-based options (above the fray, back to the garden) we must constantly play, in all seriousness, in the ever-present spaces of our political contestation. "Unlike the hopes of Frankenstein's monster," Haraway says, "the cyborg does not expect its father to save it through a restoration of the garden."

This form of thinking is utopian but not Edenic; rather, we might call it anti-anti-utopia. The usual unsustainable ambitions of utopia, often in practice violent, are tempered by a resistance to excessive cynicism, transactional reduction, and mere utilitarian logic. The private realm this form of building calls for need not be stark and sparse, as it was for the ancient Greeks, who viewed the private as the site of mere necessity, of physical maintenance for the more important things happening elsewhere: what Hannah Arendt has vividly described as public life of action.[20] (In taking this view of themselves as citizens, the ancient Greeks of course enjoyed the benefit of patriarchy and a slave-based economy, both blithely defended by Aristotle as natural.) But an excessive concern with comfort becomes self-defeating, for it robs the enjoyment of comfort of its point, and its potential role in public justification. The private realm is for solace and rest, to be sure, but at some point these inward projects must be put in service of the larger debate that shapes the whole of social space.

Without that debate, and the legitimacy it alone offers to a specific ordering of space, the private realm is mere usurpation, an act of aggression against those less fortunate. Property crimes are most often motivated by need or envy, but they also sometimes have a deeper political point. In effect the burglar or robber wants to know: Where is the justification for you having so much when someone else has so little? And that is not a question that can be answered in the comfort of your own home. There is no political dimension left in the current wave of un-private houses and logo-dominated public spaces; no sense of the commitment to a public good—a commitment that the genuinely private house, in its attention to thresholds, actually maintains. Home is a notion that must establish a relationship between private and public; it cannot be an end in itself.

The ideal of the cyborg polis must therefore be pursued in better forms. Such a polis is, in its way, not unlike the old civic republican ideal of a public space, where every citizen is a model of the whole, a kind of cybernetic network of common projects. Yet now we must be more aware than ever of the things that separate us—that otherness itself, and an awareness thereof, might be the thing that connects us most acutely. Our existing desires alone, so often convergent only on the meanest of material goods or the most limited of life projects, need to be tutored by our deeper longings, the things that lie beneath the smooth surfaces of exchange and chatter. And these may emerge only when we are confronted by the unexpected, the unfamiliar, the uncanny. So far, the reality of the new globalized ordering of space is, instead, a triumph of undirected inwardness—not a transcendent public realm, in other words, just a ceaseless and complacent celebration of pre-reflective individual desire.

We need deeper dreams than that. And yet, without the public oneiric spaces of the arcade or the square, without the people who can help us shape and articulate our wishes, we are left without places to do our dreaming. We are left without sites on which to engage each another when we awake from that dreaming and try to make our wishes real. We are left without the most basic enabling conditions of making a world worth wanting.

Architecture is a matter of modeling, and of course depends upon models—and their two-dimensional forebears, drawings—for the execution of design to build. Forgive me for indulging an architecture-model experience. The Empire State Building (ESB) remains my favorite of Manhattan's first-generation skyscrapers, with their roots in Art Deco and brilliant deployment of materials and will in what was known as "The Race for the Sky." Like any sane Modernist, I think the Seagram Building is a floating-base masterpiece, but the tough Indiana limestone exterior of the ESB, together with its soaring broad-shouldered silhouette make it enduringly exemplary, and beautifully complementary to the slimmer outline of the Chrysler Building some blocks uptown—an aesthetic conjunction that first inspired Madelon Vriesendorp to depict the two in bed together, and then moved Rem Koolhaas to use the image on early editions of his Manhattan masterpiece, *Delirious New York*.[21] This is not even to mention the extraordinary eighteen-month building time of the ESB, the crazy Depression-era financing masterminded by Al Smith, and the superlative manipulation of Hugh Ferriss's setback limits by Shreve, Lamb, and Harmon.

Anyway, one lunchtime, walking into the building to do some research, I was stopped at security. Visitors will know that the small and rather unassuming lobby of the ESB splits into those tourists just headed for the Observation Deck, site of sojourns by, among others, Charles Boyer (painter), Cary Grant (playboy), and Tom Hanks (architect!), and those seeking offices in the building itself. I was in the latter line and had, maybe unwisely, purchased a large model of the building, complete with a King Kong figure about the size of an outstretched hand, during the lunch hour. The humorless security guard said: "What the hell is that? Is that a weapon?" This was in 2005, and post-9/11 paranoia was still rampant. As I was framing what I hoped would be a suitably innocuous reply, another guard stepped in. "It's the building, dude. It's the *building.*" He turned to me. "Right?" I nodded with relief. They let me through.

It's the building. It's more than that, though. It's the building *inside the building*, a kind of *mise-en-abyme* of design and build: drawing to model to actual building to souvenir of iconic building. Inside-out becomes outside-in. I took the elevator up, imagining a miniature version of myself inside the model under my arm, trying to enter the replica with his own tiny replica of the design, and so on, and so on. Design always creates space—something like 90 percent open to 10 percent built, depending on materials and scale—but space is never idle. Space is the space of work, imagination, replication, and life.

* * *

I cannot conclude this first walk without indulging a philosopher's tic. Those of us in this odd profession have long enjoyed executing analysis via etymology. It is not always valid as a method, I know, but since I was first forced to study Latin in high school, and later learned some Greek and a bit more German, I can't forebear from hearing where words come from. *Architecture* is a noble word: it combines two supreme functions, the arch and the very idea of technique. Take the second first. In Plato's dialogues, *techné* is usually styled as *craft*, marking it off from other forms of making, such as *poiesis*, which literally means "the activity in which a person brings something into being that did not exist before."

Or, more basically, *making*. But *poiesis* gets all the glory: the association with poetry, of course, the most heavenly form of making, or the conjunction implied in mythopoeisis, the creation of myth. Poor old *techné* is reduced to fixing flat tires, plumbing, or (as often in Plato), carpentry. But these are exalted crafts, without which everyday life is impossible. *Technology* now rules our world—about which more on a later walk, memo, or non-lecture—but it would have been inconceivable to the ancient philosophers that *techné* would ever win out over *poiesis*. The creative world, the world itself, belongs to poets, not craftspeople. (I note, in passing, that there is an architecture firm in my home city of Toronto called Poeisis Architecture. Etymologically dubious, but full marks for effort.)

And yet, *techné* has won the larger day—for reasons worth exploring in our current ethical sojourn, now and later. For the moment, consider the other part of the operative world. An *arch* is obviously a basic element of building, from the ancient column and beam construction to create an opening or span, to the successive improvements of the Romanesque and Gothic variants. The Gothic and neo-Gothic arch define an entire aesthetic, from trefoil and cinquefoil to classic lancet, because the vaults and groining they allow are so immediately recognizable as church and collegiate buildings everywhere, from Notre Dame to the full-on copy architecture that decorated my own education at Toronto, Cambridge, and Yale. But why not? The gothic arch is a simple but brilliant innovation, pointing the two sides of its Romanesque forebear into a higher and more sublime shape. Yes!

But *arch* is more than just arches, as philosophers from Jacques Derrida to Karsten Harries remind us. An arch created space, an opening, a threshold; but it also the most profound form of building, the elevation of heavy material into the air. Even a basic arch, with its keystone and suspended structure, is a triumph of imagination. The column, whether Roman or Doric or Corinthian, is basic in design. It is a tree, more or less. But the arch creates *a tree house*—and that turns out to be everything. And so we are pushed back to the deep etymology of arch, which is not a design element but a first principle: *arché*, or structure as such. In fact, the word means beginning, or source, or basic action. It is rooted in the language of age—the archaic—but survives in the language of politics (autarchy, patriarchy, matriarchy, monarchy, anarchy). In my home country of Canada, there is a very special charity, founded by the amazing Jean Vanier, called L'Arche: The ark, a home for people dealing with intellectual disabilities of different kinds. Now, admittedly, L'Arche and—the Ark of the Covenant and Noah's Ark—too may not, perhaps, share the same etymology (scholarships suggests these all mean "vessel" or "shelter"), but we know that the Arc de Triomphe and its smaller cousin in Manhattan's Washington Square Park certainly are architectural arches par excellence.

And if you are keeping score at home: the *chi rho* symbol (sometimes called P-X or X-P, a shortened form of *alpha rho chi eta*, otherwise arch[22]) is an essential symbol of early Christianity, a transposition of the Greek. A different kind of arch. Beginnings are where we find them.

The etymology of the compound word *architect* says this: master builder, skilled craftsperson, first designer. The *arché* speak of origin and upstream knowledge; the *techné* speaks of execution. This is how we build, not by trial and error but by drawing on the deep, ancient well of wisdom and skill. That is how *arché* becomes *techné*, and vice versa.

Let's walk on.

2

Creating Environments

Though a building design may emerge in relative isolation, maybe enlivened by a few Indentikit humans walking on by, we all know the truth. Unless it is a blank canvas on the order of Dubai or some blasted-heath suburban or waterfront reclamation project, a given building must speak to its neighbors. There are districts ruled by a dull vernacular of pitched-roof banality where a Modernist plinth would serve the function (perhaps resented) of a flashy dandy at a country-club cocktail party. There are other realms where fitting in will be the right choice, a smooth assimilation that gives a new building grace and poise because of, not despite, the surround.

There are other places—I think here of Vlado Milunić and Frank O. Gehry's "Dancing House" in Prague (1996), known initially by some as "Fred and Ginger," after the Hollywood twinkle-toe duo— adds spice and glamour to a corner without actively disrupting the basic aesthetic flow of the region. This building dances because its semi-collapsed state calls attention to the Gothic, Baroque, and Art Deco neighbors without, as it were, turning up the music too loud. Gehry has since repudiated the "Hollywood kitsch" that inspired him, a legacy perhaps of his own Canadian origins being fetched by California film-glam, but the building keeps dancing nevertheless. It may no longer be called "Fred and Ginger" on the record, silver-screen icons, contributing dash and romance wherever they go, from a Hudson River ferry to a countryside snow shelter. Perhaps, as time goes, fewer and fewer people even get the reference? But a building, like a dancer, can make everything more romantic just by stepping out onto the floor.[1] But what is a floor, and where do we find them?

The Ethics of Architecture. Mark Kingwell, Oxford University Press (2021). © Mark Kingwell.
DOI: 10.1093/oso/9780197558546.003.0003

"All of humanity's problems," Blaise Pascal said, "stem from man's inability to sit quietly in a room alone."[2] Well, maybe: certainly there is a restlessness implied in this inability that will be instantly recognizable to us today, with phones that need constant attention, like pocket-sized infants, and Twitter feeds and Facebook profiles that demand a perpetual injection of self. Indeed, it can feel as if *there is no self* without these perpetual tendings and updatings. Can you sit alone in a room, doing nothing? One might as well ask someone to stop breathing, such torture would this be. After all, alone in a quiet room, there is only the true self for company, the dread confrontation with mortality and limit that most of us, most of the time, simply flee. We may pretend that the enemy is boredom, but in fact we have seen the enemy, and he is us.

Still, we must ask: Is there a sequel to the episode of principled interiority in that solitary room? The chamber is a scene of torture, for the restless ones at least, but presumably to some further purpose. Pascal wants us to see that our imagined problems will *dissolve* if we can tame our habitual fidgeting, our pointless longing after satisfaction when satisfaction is waiting right before us. But there are problems, humanity's problems, which will *not* be solved, or dissolved, this way. That is to say, not all of humanity's problems really do stem from the inability to sit quietly. The premise of the claim is false, or anyway one-sided.

Because some problems, such as injustice, are relational, not personal. Injustice is a condition that requires at least a dyad of actors or agencies. Likewise poverty, which is structurally ordered as a relation to possible contentment, not merely to absolute standards of comfort. (I am still impoverished, even if minimally comfortable, if I lack what everyone else has because of bad birthright luck.) While some of us steadfast ones may be able to throw off the nagging bonds of status anxiety and personal discontent—presumably the sorts of problems Pascal has in mind—it is not at all clear that such individual discipline has any lasting bearing on general social conditions. Uneven distribution of goods, the generation-spanning immiseration of social groups, and the creation of new precariats as a result of technological change—these are not the sorts of things that can simply be thought away.

So let us enhance the valence of Pascal's remark by first qualifying it, and then extending its reach. All of humanity's self-made problems may stem from the vaunted ability to sit still; but some problems, and usually the more intractable ones, require *the exercise of human agency* to be solved. They demand action, not contemplation. The quiet room remains essential to this task, however, because it is only by way of the reflection made possible by that room that we human agents will be able to bend our moral universe toward justice.

The role of the room—the actual built interior—must not be underestimated in this perpetual task. Human action takes place in public, as Hannah Arendt sagely argued, but the staging area of such action is private life: the life made possible by enclosure. The political dimensions of a room in fact are along two vectors: as launchpad, and as repository. The room creates the conditions of possibility by which I achieve active selfhood. Here, the physical interior facilitates the mental interior necessary for robust agency. By the same token, the room gives me a place to put things: like the printed word, to which it bears important metaphorical affinity, the room is a vessel of consciousness. I return here after forays into the hurly-burly of public life. Messages and lessons may be stored here for future reference. I can engage in further rounds of reflection, getting set for another sortie into public. The room, like my mind itself, a matter of recursive function, forever reflecting in a dynamic feedback loop on the very idea of itself.

To see all of this more clearly, we must go back to basics again and again, circling our targets simply because they are, too often, so obvious as to retreat from view. A room may thus be broken into three basic pieces: walls, thresholds, and affordances. Let us take each of these features in turn.

The wall is the structural, and logical, extension of the hut. The simplest hut, the physical expression of a quest for shelter, is a dugout or personal defile: a room in effect constructed out of space carved out of the earth and supplemented with whatever materials are ready to hand: sticks, rocks, bark, chunks of ice, and perhaps a stretch of leather or cloth. These last form the first important innovation of the basic hut: walls that can be carried and erected at will, in the form of tents or caravans. The transient nature of these walls need not detract from the luxury of the spaces created by them. One thinks, here, of the elaborate, even decadent tent-dwellings of some nomadic desert peoples. When the conditions of life force you to move a great deal, it makes sense to invest in a long-term solution embracing peripatetic life rather than existing in a state of denial, starting from scratch each time. (I will have more to say about huts toward the end of these ethical-architectural peregrinations, in Chapter 6.)

A miniature version of the same point illustrates the genius of the umbrella, which is of course a portable roof. And speaking of roofs, they do not in fact constitute a distinct basic element of the interior, since walls curved in the proper manner will enact the roof. Once we accept this, the ceiling or roof of a built form is just a matter of geometry. The dominant angle between wall and ceiling may be 90 degrees, but that is a matter of convention, not metaphysics. Likewise the predominant use of the same right angle between walls. But we are all acquainted with rooms where the walls join at obtuse or acute angles, or simply curve to create space.

Walls are designed, for the most part, either to keep people (and things) in or to keep people (and things) out. But there must be some passage between the inside and outside, or the wall does not serve its function. Notoriously, these passages are the weakest points in the well: the gate, the door, the portcullis. An attack from the outside will likely focus here, as will peaceful or legitimate exit and entry. A prisoner or an apostatic monk may "go over the wall" and so leave the cells inside; but the phrase itself expresses the illicitness of this form of leave-taking, just as "scaling the wall" suggests, metaphorically, the difficulty of any attempt to get inside, whatever that may mean: corporate success, gender equality, respite from poverty or misery.

Every wall must possess features of both solidness and permeability. Hence the need for thresholds.

A threshold is limit. It is both inside and outside at once, part of the interior and yet not part of it. The threshold is as much a conceptual limit as a physical one: it marks the difference in modes of existence between outside and inside. In some times and cultures, the threshold embodied purification, as we shake off the dust of exterior, public, perhaps profane life in anticipation of the interior, private, and sometimes sacred experience of the inside. The word threshold reminds us: this was a section of the floor filled regularly with clean straw—thresh—placed so that we might clean our feet, symbolically as well as literally, before full entry.

The threshold is an airlock, sometimes literally, a space of transition. We shed our outside gear, and with it our outside selves. We assume a new mode of interacting (an "inside voice") even as we assume the demands of a different mode of being. The threshold is no idle boundary; it is the physical feature that marks the enacted distinction between inside and outside. Neither of these two, each dependent conceptually upon the other, can exist without the insertion of the threshold, which is both of them and neither of them at once.[3]

To cross a threshold can be a scared act, a heroic, a threatening one: breaking and entering, penetration from by-invitation-only vampires. Thresholds are literal and conceptual and omnipresent. The most basic one for human consciousness is the material fact of the body itself, since inevitably conceived—at least sometimes—as a Cartesian vessel of our odd dualism.

The central philosophical question about the condition of embodied consciousness is not the traditional one of what we can do *about* it: solve the mind-body, kick it upstairs to the mind-brain problem, deny its power with strict materialism, what have you. No, the central philosophical question here is also the central political question: not what can we do about our personhood, but what can we do *with* it.

What makes something a *table*? In the terminology offered by ecological psychologist James J. Gibson, it is an affordance. Affordances are features of an environment that allows animals, including humans, to do things. They are elements of a physical space that support our embodiment and its many projects, large and small. Tools and weapons, corridors and walkways—all these are affordances, shaped to our needs and desires. But perhaps the most basic affordance (it is the first one Gibson mentions in his classic treatise on the subject) is a floor.[4]

So what makes a floor a floor? It must be nearly horizontal, nearly flat, rigid, and extended. Gibson says: "It is stand-on-able, permitting an upright posture for quadrupeds and bipeds. It is therefore walk-on-able and run-over-able. It is not sink-into-able like a surface of water or a swamp." Now think of a table as an elevated section of floor, raised to a height suitable to human physiognomy—about 30 inches. Once this square or rectangle or circle of floor is raised, we can extend the range of advantages bestowed by upright posture. The table (also horizontal, flat, rigid, and extended) affords us many new things.

We can place objects—the aforementioned tools and weapons, but also utensils and bowls and things to eat—close to hand and retrieve them without squatting or bending over. We can gather together to talk, plan, eat, and work—all the while remaining upright! But that is not all. The table—in its sub-form, the desk—also supports that other essential affordance of civilization, the writing surface. Add vellum or papyrus or paper, a suitable scoring instrument, and a graphematic alphabet, and you have the written word.

The written word is an extension of mind. It allows us to set down thoughts and narratives so they do not instantly vanish. Writing is a bargain with temporality, in everything from shopping lists (note to future self: buy milk) and literary or philosophical classics (we remember Plato two millennia after he became dust). A table is thus a machine for thinking, in the same sense that, as Le Corbusier said, the house is a machine for living. Many, though not all, tables are accompanied by chairs. So what is a chair? Like the table, it is an affordance—but a dangerous one. The chair looks great at first. It outlines a median position between lying down and standing up. It is, in effect, a durable structural support for the human squat, relieving the strain on our legs. We pull our body-formed chairs around the elevated-floor table.

Now we can linger over dinner, extend staff meetings beyond the boredom threshold, and continue our exercises in thought, written or not, for hours at a time. This last is perhaps best done alone. Rodin's famous sculpture, that icon of mental concentration, is of—what else—a solitary man sitting.[5]

Chairs are not universally admired. The ancient Greeks favored couches. Tailors traditionally sit cross-legged to sew. The La-Z-Boy recliner offers the dubious gift of a chair that is really a bed. By now, we all know that too much sitting can be bad for your health. Rodin's muscular Thinker acquired that physique somewhere else! Stand up, move around, stretch, fidget, maybe do some curls with the 15-pound weights. Write standing up, like Thomas Wolfe or Philip Roth or Vladimir Nabokov. (But don't write in bed, like Proust.) Or acquire a desk that elevates on command, like those in Silicon Valley workplaces. This high-tech affordance frees you from the tyranny of the fixed-height work surface and its tricky companion, the chair. Sit, stand; sit, stand; sit, stand.

Like the table, the chair is an engine of thought, but one that runs on volatile fuel: use with caution. Also, get out of the office entirely and walk. In the view of many thinkers—Aristotle was one, according to legend—true thinking is only possible while walking. But you still have to stop at some point and set down your thoughts, if you want them to last. You can do this! Commit ideas to memory as you stroll, or speak into a portable Dictaphone, or jot down notes on a portable table, otherwise known as a notebook.

These are bits of thought-storage that can be retrieved later. And then, when you are back at your upright desk, share them with the future. As Shakespeare's Sonnet 65 makes clear, the wrack of battering days, Time, itself, can destroy most things. But, under proper conditions, we witness an everyday miracle: "That in black ink my love may still shine bright."

Let us suppose, then, that the basic features of the interior are set. Now what? If the aim of human existence is to achieve robust agency, where do we go from here?

Note, first, the critical capacities of the room. It is not a neutral space. Like any part of the made world, any achievement of *techné*, the room has in-built tendencies, not all of which may be present by design. A room can be cozy, or oppressive, or austere. It can structure power relations, as in a lecture hall or office, where the array of affordances and even the walls themselves may serve a specific political purpose. A room may likewise body forth a relationship: of love and marriage (consider the so-called master bedroom), of eating and socializing, of making people wait or ushering them into intimacy. The open-plan house, like the open-plan office, is parasitic in a sometimes uncomfortable manner on this division of space into function—what architects call *program*. Those of us who have found and refined our consciousness in more divided spaces can find these vast stretches of unstructured space alien, cold, forbidding, or even creepy.

* * *

The history of the interior reminds us that this complex aspect of built culture is coextensive with the creation of modern individuality. As peoples migrate into proximity with each other, communal and semi-communal dwellings gradually give way to the idea of an isolated personal interior, the home however humble that is a person's castle. This is not merely (merely!) a matter of creating selfhood out of the mass of humanity; it is also inherently political, in the black-ink form of property rights, protections against search and seizure, and the presumptive cloak of privacy. Law serves consciousness, especially as it forms and relates to the physical facts of existence. A room is much a legal construct as it is material, social, and personal.

What goes on in these rooms? Well, recall the manner in which we began this part of our stroll about the room. Can rooms serve to bolster individual consciousness? Of course they do, and necessarily. Can they underwrite our actions in the world? Once more: of course they do, and necessarily. But how *exactly* does this work?

Heidegger reminds us that a room is always more than itself. It is a destination, say of a lecture toward which I am making my way. I am already present in the room before I get there, in the form of my expectations, cares, previous experience of the lecturer, and so on.[6] Once I arrive, matters are even more complicated, as Heidegger illustrates, for how the room is arranged, even down the most mundane detail, affects my consciousness. This is what Heidegger calls the "manifestness" of the room, and we can say that it is the most basic form of what cognitive science will come to call *extended mind*: the forms of consciousness that exceed the physical, and sometimes temporal, limits of the body.[7] Most forms of such extension are not existential-phenomenological in Heidegger's deep sense, and may employ the most everyday versions of technological and cognitive aids. But these forms of everydayness are themselves, of course, suffused with ontological significance.

Note, further, that Heidegger's examples are as much attuned to failure as to success, and address affordances within the room. This gives special poignancy to, for example, finding yourself in the wrong seat in that same lecture room. Now I might experience what Heidegger calls "unreadyness-to-hand": a kind of failed relationship to a room. I can't see the blackboard if the room is set in tiers of seats, or I must move awkwardly to write upon it if I am the one giving the lecture. The position of the board within the room "is not a determinacy of the board, like its black colour," Heidegger says, "but a determinacy that is merely relative to us who are here in this very situation. This determinate quality of the board—its bad position—is not a so-called objective property but is relative to the subject." This nonobjective relation is complex, however. The board "is not badly positioned in relation to us who are factically to be found here, rather the board is badly positioned in this lecture room. [If] we think of the room not as tiered, but as a dance hall, then the board would be sitting quite favourably in the corner, out of the way."[8]

Typically we forget, ignore, or take for granted these relationships *precisely because* of the proximity between my sense of self and the various objects, times, and spaces with which I interact. So I may use a cane to extend my perceptual mind in space, or compose a reminder note, a grocery list perhaps, and put it somewhere to remind (apt word!) my future self of my past self's needs. And I may think very little is at stake in doing so. All technology, especially the communications media that so dominate our own experience of failing to sit in rooms quietly alone, may be viewed, in this manner, as what Marshall McLuhan called "extensions of man."[9]

Heidegger likewise reminds us, in his trenchant critique of technology, that we make a mistake if we focus on the products of technology rather than the conceptual surround it creates, the immensely powerful assumption of standing reserve and *enframing*, through which the whole of the world is cast in terms of its status as a resource awaiting consumption. This includes obvious features of the world such as natural things, the way a forest may be viewed as potential lumber, but also our own desires, time, and even the very idea of existence. We can only challenge the power of this way of viewing ourselves and the world by thinking technology through. Which involves, naturally, thinking about thinking itself.[10]

Almost all of what passes for discourse about technology cannot be realistically counted as such thinking. In failing to question technology in its essence, it fails to reveal our own. Heidegger's own poetic call to arms at the end of his most famous discussion the question are worth quoting: "The closer we come to the danger [of our relationship to enframing], the more brightly do the ways into the saving power begin to shine and the more questioning we become. For questioning is the piety of thought."[11]

Let us conclude this part of our general ethical reflections—which, by their nature, are always themselves *preliminary to action*—by pausing to consider the nature of interiority itself, in all its aspects. An inside can only exist because there is an outside—see *thresholds*, earlier in this chapter. More to the larger point, the interior of something is its beating heart, the hidden chamber that pumps lifeblood through the entire organism. (We speak of the chambers of the heart, not always noting the domestic-architectural resonance of the usage.) The interior life of a human existence is more essential, more intimate than anything else about it—even considering the various extensions of mind that we associated with mediated life, the trails of messages and feeds and posted images. And now note this: we cannot have this interior without its proper enabling conditions. There is no public without the private. An interior life, sustained by an interior structure—a room—is indispensable for the human experiment.

There are no individuals without interiors. It follows that there can be no individual action, no quest for justice or fairness—though likewise there no drive to serial killing or revenge—without the double-sustaining function of the room. The physical interior mirrors, and sustains, the mental interior. We cannot imagine one without the other. The age-old philosophical and ethical question: What is it *to be me*? In large measure, it is to find myself somewhere in particular, in this place or that, in a specific room. Where else?

And from here I launch my projects of self, my hopes and dreams, my aspirations to duty or happiness or simple survival. That is the nature of the human consciousness, at once mysterious and all too familiar. Here we are, you and I. Our problems are not entirely of our own making. What shall we do about them? Let me think, let me think!

Indeed. And so now, moving out of the interior, think of Aldo Rossi's indispensable study of landmark buildings, or monuments.[12] Some monuments are obvious: the Parthenon, the Arc de Triomphe, the Statue of Liberty. These speak directly, if controversially, to the deep meaning of orienting structures: memory, commemoration, recalling. But other buildings, Rossi reminds us, serve what we might call secular or incidental monumentality. Everyone can likely name a building in any given city that has become monumental, even if its execution is quite modest. I think of the Parker House in Boston, planted near the State House and the Common, not far from the moving Saint-Gaudens bas-relief sculpture of Colonel Robert Gould Shaw taking his African American men of the 54th Union Regiment into Civil War battle. That is a monument, and not just because Jack Kennedy and Jackie Onassis stayed there, and ate the famous Parker House rolls with their bowls of clam chowder.

No, it's because it anchors a corner. And speaking of corners, how about the Corner House in Manhattan's West Village, an unassuming restaurant that looms large in people's imaginations because of Bloody Marys and burgers. Or the White Horse Tavern, not far away, where Dylan Thomas drank himself into oblivion and, eventually, his sad demise? When I lived in the West Village, these were my hangouts—though of late they are too touristy, with long sidewalk lines to get into the Corner House. The Palmer House in Chicago, right inside The Loop, is more impressive than the crazy Monadnock Building (named for a New Hampshire mountain, and built by two different architects), and for me more iconic than the towering SOM Sears, Willis, Hancock Towers, or whatever the names are now. The CN Tower in Toronto, the tallest building in the world until it was surpassed in 2007 by the (then-named) Burj Khalifa; but also the Eaton Centre, with its iconic public-art installation of Michael Snow floating geese, and the otherwise punishing SkyDome, which also features Michael Snow artwork. The Bidendum in London is maybe more beloved than any of the usual suspects—Saint Paul's, Big Ben, the Eye. The Eiffel Tower in Paris, sure, but notoriously Guy de Maupassant ate lunch there every day so he would not have to look at it.

Then: The arch in St. Louis. The Jin Mao tower in Shanghai. Taipei 101 in Taiwan. The Sydney Opera House in Australia. The Heart of Midlothian in Edinburgh (not a building, not even a statue, just a paved marker on the Royal Mile, on which people regularly spit for good luck). The Coit Tower in San Francisco, at once mocked and revered in Alfred Hitchcock's oneiric film *Vertigo* (1958). Antoni Gaudí's Sagrada Família in Barcelona. Naturally you will have your own list of such things, drawn from your own experience. That's what the lifeworld is like! The basic point is simply this: landmarks, or monuments, come in all shapes and sizes: tall structures, sure; but also sticking points, crossroads, memory-wells, desire-sinks. We are drawn to *place* in a variety of narratives and means. Buildings both guide that and teach it: they are beacons.

Consider one small example with a fair bit of background detail. The statue in the center of London's Piccadilly Circus, usually called Eros, is relatively small in stature. It includes a fountain and bronze and copper stepped pediment. In fact it is not a depiction of Eros but rather of his twin brother Anteros, the demi-god of requited or returned love. (By contrast, Eros is desire *simpliciter*, unrestrained and promiscuous.) The work was commissioned to sculptor Alfred

Gilbert in 1886 as a monument to the life of social reformer Anthony Ashley Cooper, seventh Earl of Shaftesbury (1801–1885). Cooper's forebear, the third earl (1671–1713), under the very same name and title, was the author of landmark works on the aesthetics of beauty and taste.[13] The statue's model was a fifteen-year-old studio assistant to Gilbert. It was the first statue in London to be cast in aluminum. It bankrupted Gilbert, whose 3,000-pound commission evaporated in construction overruns.

The statue was controversial from its reveal, and has since been vandalized and eulogized in about equal measure. Its mistaken association with Eros has made the fountain, once intended for drinking, into a landmark for sexual rendezvous, especially *sub rosa* homosexual hook-ups. Fun fact: when I was a very young man visiting London for the first time, I was propositioned by a middle-aged man as I sat on its steps. Further fun fact: the Anteros figure holds a bow but it is lacking an arrow, thus prompting the idea that the *shaft* is *buried* somewhere else. Ha ha. There are four versions in total, actually, which seems to create a kind of global Eros/Anteros economy (one of the copies is in Australia). The statue has been moved, decorated, and made into a snow globe for Christmas.[14]

All of this for one rather small monument in the global system of structure. Consider the obvious example of the Empire State Building in Manhattan. It is of course iconic, monumental, inescapable. It has appeared in countless films and televisions shows, even in songs by wildly diverse composers and singers.[15] This is not even to mention the stupefying yet mesmerizing eight-hour-and-five-minute film by Andy Warhol (1964), a work that simply records without commentary or camera movement the *existence* of the building from one evening to 3 a.m. the next morning. A central aspect of the current argument is that these qualities, as Warhol understood, make the physical building *hard to see*.[16] It is almost too present. Even Andy Warhol's notorious multi-hour film of the building, in which nothing happens, fails to rescue this monument from looming invisibility.

The building then becomes a font of metaphors and likelihoods: New York's lighthouse (Robert A. M. Stern), the syringe of Manhattan (Martin Amis), the lonely and inexplicable sphinx (F. Scott Fitzgerald), the comic-book fortress of Kavalier and Clay (Michael Chabon).

But there can still be, as it were, a kind of contextual excavation of the physical building: the narrative of its blindingly fast construction, its role in skyline conceptions of New York and urbanism more generally, its place in the history of tall buildings. Even the title of my own book about the Empire State Building—*nearest thing to heaven*—is borrowed from films that feature the monumentality of the Empire State: *An Affair to Remember* (1957, d. Leo McCarey, with Cary Grant and Deborah Kerr) and *Love Affair* (1939, also d. Leo McCarey, with Irene Dunne and Charles Boyer).

The statue in Piccadilly Circus may be of Anteros, not Eros, but monuments establish and perpetuate what a Freudian would call *erotic exchanges*. They live in and through our individual desires. Not all of those desires are conscious ones, not do they reliably align with facts. In some very real sense, the statue is of Eros because it materializes the erotic. It is a *node of cathexis*, or desire-investment.

But to continue this walk to its logical ending, we must now consider some additional factors in the ethics of environment. A building may establish itself as a monument, and therefore organize or orient an environment. But an environment is both life-world and matter, a mixture of phenomenology and the hard palettes of material construction.

* * *

When we consider the future evolution of cities, and the buildings that anchor them, we must always be aware of this architectural version of the mind-body problem bequeathed to all humans since Descartes but, indeed, rooted in older Christian, Greek, and Buddhist traditions. What is spirit or soul, and what is body or matter? These are highly abstract philosophical and theological debates, but they have very real design implications under current conditions.

Here we confront the notion of "smart buildings." The positive version of this idea, based in technological optimism that is always already open to question, is that there may be forms of construction that integrate old-fashioned material deployments—bricks, mortar, concrete, steel, glass—with algorithmic software that allows an otherwise mute structure to become interactive. At the time of this writing, the dominant theme for such "smartness" is linked to the Internet of Things (IoT), the general thesis and emergent practice of everyday objects becoming responsive to human needs and interests. Thus, for example, a refrigerator that lets you know when you are running low on staple groceries, a television that preprograms your favorite shows, or a security system that you can voice access from anywhere to check on the children or the cats.

Many opponents of IoT, especially in these domestic settings, note the surveillance possibilities that lurk behind alleged conveniences or affordances. If your fridge knows where you are, what you eat, and what you need, are these not data points that might be whisked away and sold or otherwise manipulated, just as your online shopping preferences and social media interactions have been? Allegedly private or individual life is thereby reduced to a kind of human grazing field, where the biological entities feed on the hay of desire even as their behavior (if not their actual flesh!) is harvested for potential profit.

A smart building, and by extension a smart city, poses the same issues on a larger scale. One can even imagine nightmare scenarios here, on the order of tech-gone-rogue narratives we have seen in everything from Stanley Kubrick's *2001: A Space Odyssey* (1968) to the *Terminator* franchise (1984; et seq.). In Philip Kerr's 1991 novel *The Gridiron*, a smart building—complete with voice-activated commands, holographic servants, and self-cleaning protocols— achieves something like consciousness and decides to eliminate its creators, and some of its tenants, in an attempt to procreate. In biblical fashion, Kerr's fictional frame calls the original AI of the building *Abraham* and its programmed "sons" *Isaac* and *Ishmael*.

Killer buildings, like killer robots, are the stuff of bad dreams and paranoia. But one need not be a deranged Luddite to wonder if real-world applications of technology to architecture and city planning are a good thing. On the one hand, we can see the benefit of developments such as Hudson Yards in Manhattan or Sidewalk in Toronto for shopping, entertainment, and even traffic easements.

Cities around the world, including Berlin, Shanghai, Dubai, and Singapore, are racing each other to become "smarter," that is, more integrated between the hardware of built environments and the software of the algorithmic surround.

The ethical issues for architects here are not always entirely clear. Wishing to serve clients and potential tenants of a given building might suggest that integrated IoT technology is a clear gain: instead of being blank pieces of matter, buildings become responsive surrounds for my desires and purposes. On the other hand, that very same technological integration facilitates surveillance, control, and constraint. Not least, at every moment data are being gathered by the algorithms for redeployment, and perhaps profit, somewhere else. Tenants are transformed from agents into products, sources of information and revenue.

Hence the ground-level opposition to many developments, especially when the urban project is clearly associated with a tech behemoth such as Google, already the most efficient data-gathering project the world has ever witnessed.

When we walk through a neighborhood of smart buildings, when we enter and exit an edifice that records everything we might say or do, it is not paranoid to wonder if this is for our benefit or for someone else's. The state? The corporation? The developers of future, even smarter algorithms?

We cannot know. What we can recall is that Walter Benjamin's celebrated *flâneur*, the open-minded sage of the arcades, more and more becomes instead a prisoner of an advanced version of Michel Foucault's carceral society, surveilled and self-surveilled in the panopticon of ubiquitous technology.[17] Buildings are only part of this new surround. If you are carrying a smartphone in your pocket, all this may be moot already.

Walk on, perhaps at a quicker pace! Not that anyone will follow this advice, but you might just want to *ditch your phone*, like a gangster tossing a burner down a sewer grate. Ah, but now it is the building that is watching you. This is community not of shared solitudes, but of shared visibilities ...

3

Creating Communities

Let's begin this walk with a brisk theoretical briefing. I think we
cannot conceive of communities, especially as experienced physically in neighborhoods and cities, without considering the very profound human issue of *risk*. Because this is not strictly or obviously
an architectural category, beyond the usual constraints of building
code and safety mechanisms, allow a little latitude on the discussion
as stroll from one neighborhood to another, perhaps crossing some
risk thresholds as we go.

What are the political dimensions of risk? I will argue here that
there are three distinct orders of political risk, and that they are
nested in ways that have been neglected by urban theory, traditional political theory, and public policy alike. Only by disentangling
and then seeing the complex nesting of these risk orders will we be
able to appreciate the role that risk plays in geopolitical, especially
urban, life.

The most obvious order of risk is surely the consequences
generated by at-risk populations around the globe. For obvious
historical and political reasons, large chunks of the Earth's population daily face material challenges unknown to the rest of the
world, especially in its blessed "Western" reaches. Food security, for
example—the ability to count on regular and affordable supplies of
daily sustenance—is a concern so far from the minds of even the
poorest North Americans and Europeans that it can be difficult to
imagine life in sub-Saharan Africa or parts of Asia.

Potable water is an even more vivid example, since even the most
privileged among the planet's seven billion human inhabitants
now realize that a continued supply of fresh and nontoxic water

The Ethics of Architecture. Mark Kingwell, Oxford University Press (2021). © Mark Kingwell.
DOI: 10.1093/oso/9780197558546.003.0004

is imperiled. The tainted-water scandals in Flint, Michigan, and Walkerton, Ontario, are timely, if also nasty, reminders of how fragile the global freshwater table is even in the developed world. Elsewhere, the scandal is a daily reality. Physical risks of this sort pose associated dangers over supply and control. Violence is more prevalent in nations where resource scarcity is an ongoing problem.[1]

And so those persons who find themselves living under such conditions have traditionally felt that they have legitimate demands on those with the resources to alleviate actual and possible harms. This is the moral basis of claims for disaster relief, poverty and disease control, food security, and reduction of yawning wealth inequality. Let's call this cluster of issues *Order-One Risk*.

But there is already a hint of another dimension of risk in play here. The inhabitants of risky populations and areas did not choose their positions; it is the result of a particularly nasty feature of what is known as the *birthright lottery*. Where and who I am born to be is a matter of luck, but it is luck of an especially far-reaching kind. Thus, further upstream of these urgent questions of relief and aid is another dimension of risk, concerning the distribution of risk itself. What are the politics involved?

Well, first, most risks can be divided into the chosen and the unchosen. In contrast to other situations where choice is a factor in human affairs, when it comes to the basic situation of life—where and who I am—we tend to discount chosen risk and inflate unchosen risk. That is, we tend to minimize aid or even punish those who suffer from the outcomes of risky choices, and help or at least consider helping those shouldering the burdens of unchosen risk. So, for example, we typically have little sympathy for a gambler or property speculator who went all-in on some chancy bet, and ended up losing. "Tough luck," we say, implying that the bad luck was, in effect, purchased by the speculator or gambler as a matter of conscious agency.

But when risk is distributed both unevenly and without consent, we think it right to favor the unfavored. Someone who had the no-fault misfortune to be born in a degraded environment with imminent prospects of struggle and violence, we do not usually—unless we are ruthless to the point of cynicism—call that tough luck. We call it, instead, misfortune, and consider it to have some moral traction on us. The gambler has no one to blame for himself, we think, unless we subscribe to social influence or addiction theories of a far-reaching kind.

But even the addiction narrative usually involves elements of choice and responsibility—we do not, as when Homer Simpson observes the breakdown of wife Marge in a Vegas gambling spree, blame an interior monster called "Gamblor," who has taken possession of her soul. If addiction is a monster, it is a metaphorical one, and thus a beast we believe can be slain through a combination of guidance, contextual support, and willpower. Hence the most sympathetic observer of someone taking bad risks by choice will likely insist that there is always a measure of personal responsibility in play, even in those cases where robust personal autonomy has been partially compromised. Gamblers are not automatons, and choice matters even when it is complicated.[2]

By contrast, when there is no matter of choice in play—where, in fact, there cannot be—even the most grim observer will have a hard time maintaining that the risk incurred is a matter of personal responsibility. Central to this issue is not just the fact but *the supreme power* of birthright lottery. The overarching fact of human existence is that we do not choose who and where we are born, nor do we choose most of the consequences of those facts. This lottery—captured by the notion of "tell me who your parents are and I will tell you who you are"—governs the bulk of life chances for all humans. Let's call this *Order-Two Risk*, since it generates many (or most) of the conditions considered in any discussion of Order-One Risk.

Order-Two Risk can be spectral. What I mean is that smokescreens of various kinds work to conceal its political essence. For example, if you had the "good sense" to be born to wealthy parents in the developed world, your chances of comfort, long life, and happiness are maximized. You might even begin to think that this highly contingent outcome is something you engineered out of personal virtue. Thus the spectacle of Excessive Entitlement Disorder (sometimes also called "affluenza") whereby a lucky sod is born on third base and grows up thinking he hit a triple. Good luck is here comprehensively confused with virtue.

That baseball-derived metaphor was often used to describe former US President George W. Bush. This mediocre scion of a powerful family attended Yale University as a "legacy" applicant—itself a traditional practice of preference that functions as a sort of frequent-flier program for the wealthy who convert their cash, in the form of reliable donations, into cachet, in the form of an Ivy League degree (I won't say education). But more than this, Bush entered the White House as president of the United States, despite being drastically underqualified, because of a network of influence that, in another context, would have landed him a comfortable chair on the New York Stock Exchange. Indeed, from the point of view of the Bush family circle, the two offices are more or less the same thing.

Such influence peddling is offensive all by itself, but is made exponentially worse by the delusion that the resulting success was somehow earned rather than granted. There is no virtue in being born to rich parents, any more than there is vice in being born to poor ones. But these obvious facts can be hard to see through the mists of delusion that settle around wealth and power. This is the essence of Randian entitlement, that bizarre stew of anti-collectivism and aggressive individualism that suffuses the tortuous novels already discussed. Success is purely the result of individual creativity and effort, parasitically drained by the forces of altruism, taxation, and the general good. Never mind that, in fact, there is no such success without markets, and workers, and the infrastructure that makes economies possible—not least the baseline existence of money, that collective fantasy token of trust and cooperation.

More recently, the same phenomenon of transmuting inherited wealth into personal virtue can be observed in Donald Trump. The Republican presidential candidate liked to portray himself as a self-made man, even a man of the people, conveniently obliterating the fact that this worldly success was made possible by a hefty inheritance. The *New Yorker* satirist Andy Borowitz nailed the point with an imagined news article headlined "Trump Economic Plan Calls for Every American to Inherit Millions from Father." According to the article, Trump made a rallying speech about the economy: " 'There are people at my rallies, desperate people, desperate because they want jobs,' he told his luncheon audience at the Detroit Economic Club. 'Once they inherit millions from their father, they will never want a job again.' "[3]

Such extreme cases are targets of easy satire. But political theorists have struggled with birthright lottery, in large measure because its contingencies seem so intractable. How could one ever hope to stem the tide of consequences brought about by the brute facts of birth and situation? Every post-facto justice measure would be climbing uphill against the steep grade of chance. And are we perhaps overstepping the bounds of legitimate intervention if we try to advance such measures? Perhaps there are simply some things that remain misfortunes rather than injustices?

But every conceivable distinction between misfortune and injustice is open to criticism. Is the New Orleans flood, say, merely an act of god (misfortune) or a matter of heinously bad infrastructure (injustice)? When does inept government count more than the simple bad luck of living in a drowned parish?

To answer these thorny questions, many people follow the lead of John Rawls's foundational work on justice, and have adopted versions of an "original position." This is an imagined choice scenario in which the specific circumstances of birth are excluded by a "veil of ignorance," thus freeing choosers to settle on schemes of justification and basic social structure that are fair to all.[4] Note that, when we imagine what rules of the social game we might choose if we didn't know who our parents are, the basic lottery is assumed. The uneven natural distribution of favors is what makes justice an issue in the first place.

Some critics have balked at the idea of such ignorance-based choice as the basis of legitimate social policy, but consider for a moment the core insight. If I don't know who, in particular, I am, then I really do have a basic rational stake in upholding practices of fairness in distributing goods and life chances. A simple analogy captures the point. Suppose I am asked by my mother to cut the remaining portion of a pie into two sections, one for me and one for my brother. The catch is that, while I *cut* first, he gets to *choose* first. The only rational action on my part is to opt for equal shares of the remaining pie. Any other course is self-defeating, given an assumption of basic rationality on the part of my brother (i.e., he will choose the larger piece, given the chance). The original position in effect models a complex version of this scenario: we all can do the cutting, but nobody knows who's going to get to do the choosing.

But here I want to postulate yet another order of risk. It brings together the luck of the lottery with the original-choice model's notion of consenting participants, but with a new twist. This *Order-Three Risk* concerns the relative levels of *aversion* and *tolerance* regarding risk itself, qualities that might themselves be distributed unevenly within a population. Indeed, all evidence shows that the distribution of tolerance to risk is wildly uneven. Some people are simply more inclined to take chances—to shoulder risk—than others. Moreover, they consider this risky behavior rational.

This is neither a matter of brute injustice in circumstances, nor a function of the (closely related) chances of who our parents are. In other words, Order-Three Risk is distinct from both Order-One and Order-Two Risks because it concerns individual orientation to risk in general. It is an independent personal relationship to chance that can, under certain circumstances, govern significant outcomes for other people.

How so? Well, imagine, once again, that we are in an original-choice position such as Rawls's thought experiment. Some people might opt for unequal outcomes, on the chance that they would enjoy the fruits of inequality. They gamble on the benefits of unfair distribution working in their favor.

In this way, risk-tolerant participants in the choice game can skew results in favor of social rules that allow steep inequalities, with no welfare floor. These players may lose their gamble, of course; but meanwhile *everybody* loses because the game is skewed against fairness. And this is exactly what obtains in the so-called real world. Neoliberal economics dominate life and choice, favoring the favored while maintaining a narrative of *possible* success for others—the American Dream or some similar bill of goods.

Once more, we could solve this problem by theoretically ruling aversion and tolerance out of the ideal situation. Attitude to risk (we might argue), in common with other personal factors such as height or physical beauty, must be excluded from one's self-knowledge under the conditions of ideal choice. This will clear the way for rational agreement about society's basic structure.

But this move looks merely ad hoc, and therefore unjustified. More significantly, these behind-the-veil risk-positive people are just idealized cousins to the free-market risk-takers of the actual world, those who believe that they deserve larger outcomes because of what they have ventured. Such people don't believe they were born on third base; they believe they took a chance on a hanging off-speed pitch and hustled their way to that triple.

We can understand the significance of Order-Three Risk better by bringing it into even closer relation to the other two orders of risk. If risk aversion and risk tolerance are themselves part of the birthright lottery, not pure personal virtues, the game changes. Cheerleaders for "entrepreneurship" and "innovation" love to argue that risk tolerance is an admirable cultivated quality, like courage or temperance (even if often ventured with other people's money). But what if it is more an inherited tendency and, as such, a morally vacuous feature, like height or beauty? This "essential" quality of self might be just as much a matter of who your parents are as whether you were born in happy Denmark or benighted sub-Saharan Africa.

This in turn suggests that the distribution of attitude to risk—Order-Three Risk—demands justice consideration. We might need to *control for*, rather than merely assume, the uneven distributions of willingness to take chances. Indeed, if such distributions are having negative systemic effects at the widest level, reinforcing schemes of governance that favor risk tolerance, we should view regulation of Order-Three Risk as a central tenet of any just society. We can tolerate marginal gains scored by those who are physically attractive, or athletically blessed (Giselle Bündchen and Tom Brady are simply going to be better off than most people, given the world as we find it), but we would certainly not want such features to govern general outcomes of life chances for everyone. Risk tolerance might be just as adventitious, and so just as irrelevant.

The political conclusion becomes evermore obvious: risk is a matter for justice interventions at all conceptual levels. Loosening the sense of "deserved" connection between personal qualities such as risk tolerance and good outcomes is just as important as alleviating the consequences of Order-One Risk. Without both aspects, any attempt to realize justice concerning the consequences of birthright lottery will be hampered. Such attempts will fail to address the ongoing sense among the favored that they—and hence others—have what they have by right, and so that those less favored likewise deserve poor outcomes generated by the current arrangement.

In one clear and traditional sense, justice means to favor the unfavored, giving aid where it is called for. But perhaps to be more complete, justice also demands that we unfavor the favored. The core lesson is actually an old and familiar one, with new and renewed urgency. It is not enough to comfort the afflicted; we must also afflict the comfortable.

* * *

Let's finish up this particular walk by noting a few things that may or may not obvious when it comes to the ethics of architecture. The first is that architecture is never far from urban planning and urban geography. Nor, indeed, from public policy concerning these. So, for example, when we consider gentrification, neighborhood improvement, and rises in prosperity, there are demonstrable connections between the built environment and the human inhabitation of it. First, research shows that neighborhoods with larger proportions of college-educated residents are much more likely to see overall improvements in physical appearance. Likewise, second, it appears evidential that districts with good initial appearance—intact façades, historic markers, cherished buildings—are more likely to see further improvements on this good first-based position. And third, it is very likely that areas close to central business districts and busy downtowns, in particular if these feature amenity-based constructions such as bars and restaurants, even art galleries and shops, are more likely to witness continual upticks in appearance and, of course, wealth.[5]

The opposite conclusions are implied: neighborhoods that *lack* these same criteria are more likely witness not only aesthetic degradation but also rising levels of crime, vandalism, and alienation. In effect, the recent science merely bears out the arguments made decades ago about the "broken windows" decline.[6] This is no more than Jane Jacobs backed with science and sociological research.

We might consider, before leaving these neighborhoods going up or down, the influence of Le Corbusier's urban architecture principles on issues of safety and community. Famously, his *Ville Contemporaine* plan, sometimes known as the "City for Three Million," was intended to solve problems of overcrowding, expensive housing, and urban stress. The design is bold and vivid, indeed essential: no student of architecture, amateur or professional, does not possess a mental image of the cruciform residential towers and their ideally park-like base sites. This is, perhaps, the inspiration for Howard Roark's version of solving a public-housing crisis in *The Fountainhead*; indeed, the designs revealed in the film version, as mentioned, bear a close resemblance.

But as everyone certainly knows, the material attempts to realize this vision in places as diverse as Sao Paulo and London housing developments to the Bronx and Saint James Town or North York, in Toronto, have been largely unsuccessful, if not disastrous. The vertical communities of the towers too often destroy the lived reality of the ground. It goes from playground to battleground: risk sent to the baseline of entry and exit. Then, in addition, infrastructural dysfunctions by turns disrupt the tower: elevators out of order; stairwells full of detritus, syringes, or human waste; fires, water, or electrical outages. (All of the last happened within the last year, in a residential tower community I walk through every day on my way to and from work.)

One of the most vivid depictions of the challenges posed by this architectural plan as a lived reality is an oddly hopeful one, and pursued in oddly unexpected narrative form as well. The space-alien invasion film *Attack the Block* (d. Joe Cornish, 2011) is a story of young people living in one of London's "council blocks," a barely functional sort-of-Corbusier tower of public housing just barely hanging on to the fringes of English society. There are drugs and crime and vast unhappiness here. But, as so often, when there is an external threat, internal differences gloss into resolve: the neighborhood kids, formerly gang-style rivals, league together to improvise a resistance to the unwelcome visitors. Insecurity becomes solidarity.

I have no idea if this is what it takes to resolve issues of architecture and risk. It is fiction, after all, and science fiction at that. But . . . well, some designs never leave the sketchbook or the CAD station. Or they get reproduced in a fancy journal somewhere. I had friends in grad school who thought getting a design published was far superior to having it "merely" built.[7] But some designs do get built, and some people have to live in the results. That's a whole different notion of risk.

As I completed this walk, mostly in my head of course, I came across a newspaper article about the complicity between extremely high-level architects with repressive, anti-environmental, homophobic, or otherwise objectionable political regimes. The writer called this tangle "the despot dilemma."[8]

We all know that builders have long been suborned to suspicious, even evil, state interests. What fascinates now is the double-speak into which top-line architects have been indoctrinated. Examples:

Bjarke Ingels, described here sarcastically as "self-styled seer of a progressive world" and "big tech's cheeky go-to boy," is shown smiling beside Brazil's Jair Bolsonaro, the Donald Trump of Brazil, responsible for vast environmental degradation in the burning of South American rainforests as well as being a proud homophobe and ethnic nationalist. "They've pioneered this incredible barefoot light-impact environment," Ingels said, somewhat bizarrely. "It's a model of tourism development that doesn't replace the forest or the sand, but strengthens and preserves it. It's a very welcome alternative to the kind of high-rise hotels that spring up on the beach in many places."

Um, okay? Ingels was also engaged in projects with the Saudi Arabian state to create large projects, including a new leisure resort city called Qiddiya, 45 kilometers from Riyadh, billed as a new "capital of entertainment." Reports also mentioned a confidential Saudi project that Ingels described as "a human-made ecosystem that is as close to a utopia as you dare imagine." Questioned about this engagement with the regime that evidently sanctioned the 2018 murder and subsequent capital-punishment show-trial concerning journalist Jamal Khashoggi, Ingels said "I do sincerely believe that the urban transformation of Saudi Arabia that we're taking part in is part of paving a path to a clearly needed social and cultural reform of the country." And then: "The road to ethical impact as an architect is to [propose] the future we want to companies and governments," he says, "even if they have different views. We have to embrace our differences if we want to create a future that is different."

Again, okay—I guess? But that sounds like protesting way too much, and was mocked once more as sounding "like a TED talk for dictators." There are similar accusations against French architect Jean Nouvel, in particular for his design of the Louvre Abu Dhabi, which featured prominently in a Ryan Reynolds Netflix action-thriller film called *6 Underground* (2019, d. Michael Bay—who else?). And likewise for I. M. Pei, who designed the Museum of Islamic Art in Doha, Qatar—a building I have visited—or Rem Koolhaas, who has worked extensively in China; and Zaha Hadid, who notoriously said, "I have nothing to do with workers" when it was pointed out that her design for a stadium to host the 2022 Football World Cup was being constructed in a city where hundreds of migrant workers have died on-site.

It happens that, on the same visit to Doha where I enjoyed the cool interior of Pei's museum and its astonishing Islamic artifacts, I also got lost one night walking on foot and found myself among a large group of these workers. Most of them are Indian or Pakistani, and they come to the Middle East to earn money that they send back home to impoverished families, hoping for a better step up. They live lonely bachelor lives, and have young-old faces. Their pop-up streetside markets are trading places for dog-eared Bollywood postcards and sad pirated DVDs of old movies and music videos.

Finding myself there, with no phone and no cab back to my own luxury hotel, I was at once desperate to leave and longing to stay.

I do not judge here. I suppose I am myself an intellectual globe-trotter of a certain vintage, luckier than most. But I hope I do not fool myself during these peregrinations to give lectures and conduct seminars. The *Guardian* writer Oliver Wainwright concludes this way: "Whenever the topic of ethics comes up, most architects who work in repressive climates believe their projects can transcend the abuses of the host regimes and make everyday life a bit better for the people who live there. The dilemma is whether to boycott or engage. Should a well-intentioned architect avoid working with any system they disagree with—or hope that the conditions of workers, or freedom of speech, might be improved by using their platform to raise these issues?"

That dilemma is as old as ethics itself. You must decide.

Meanwhile, we walk on.

4
Creating Art

Perhaps the most famous, certainly most quoted, dictum about beauty and architecture is that of Le Corbusier, often repeated in the course of *Vers une Architecture*: "Architecture being the masterly, correct and magnificent play of masses brought together in light, the task of the architect is to vitalize the surfaces which clothe these masses," he wrote in 1923, "but in such a way that these surfaces do not become parasitical, eating up the mass and absorbing it to their own advantage: the sad story of our present work."[1]

Together with his insistence on the primordiality of "the regulating line"—which "is a guarantee against wilfulness" and "brings satisfaction to the understanding"[2]—the recurring mantric invocation of masterly, correct, and magnificent play of masses brought together in light become shorthands for the Corbusian aesthetic—which is also, necessarily, an ethic. These are always warning shots across the Modernist bow when we consider the role of beauty in architecture, and especially the even trickier meta-issue of the *ethics* of aesthetics of architecture.

I have noted already that, for many practitioners, the notion of aesthetic *style* in building design opens up boggy ground—this despite the fact that one of the most influential movements in twentieth-century architecture is the International Style, and the equally salient fact that nobody chokes on the use of terms such as "Art Deco style," "neo-classical style," "neo-Gothic style," or even "postmodern style"—though it may remain unclear what that last one indicates. These shorthands for a given aesthetic orientation and its standard building techniques, including choice or arch or façade, are commonplace in basic architectural discourse.

The Ethics of Architecture. Mark Kingwell, Oxford University Press (2021). © Mark Kingwell.
DOI: 10.1093/oso/9780197558546.003.0005

I think that what people are wary of, when they grow cautious around style-talk, is the idea of a distinctive, perhaps too-distinctive personal style; and likewise the reliance on frothy nonfunctional doodads festooned on the basic structure of a building. Thus Witold Rybczynski, in *The Look of Architecture*, begins with a famous remark of Le Corbusier's: styles, he avers, "are to architecture what a feather is on a woman's head; it is sometimes pretty, though not always, and never anything more."[3] Rybczynski goes on, in his short and engaging book, to take issue with this typical *pronunciamento*, arguing persuasively that style is essential to understanding architecture practice and, especially, appreciation. He praises Philip Johnson for acknowledging that "A style is not a set of rules or shackles, as some of my colleagues seem to think. A style is a climate in which to operate, a springboard to leap further into the air."[4]

Rybczynski then goes on, in his short and engaging book, to take issue with this characteristic offhand claim, arguing persuasively that style is essential to understanding architecture practice and, especially, appreciation. He praises Philip Johnson for acknowledging that "A style is not a set of rules or shackles, as some of my colleagues seem to think. A style is a climate in which to operate, a springboard to leap further into the air." Rybcznski notes the ironic fact that, despite protestations, architects are in fact obsessed with style, from their self-presentation (kooky eyeglasses, basic-black wardrobes, fetishizing of Mont Blanc Meisterstück fountain pens, etc.); and quotes with approval Oscar Wilde's characteristic dictum that "In matters of importance, style is everything."[5]

Le Corbusier himself, in *Vers une architecture*, had offered this familiar, more nuanced declaration (often repeated with variations, and note the staccato, almost poetic, diction employed here for rhetorical emphasis):

> A grand epoch has begun.
> There exists a new spirit.
> There exists a mass of work conceived in the new spirit; it is to
>   be met with particularly in industrial production.
> Architecture is stifled by custom.

> The "styles" are a lie.
> Style is a unity of principle animating all the work of an epoch,
>   the result of a state of mind which has its own special
>   character.
> Our own epoch is determining, day by day, its own style.
> Our eyes, unhappily, are unable yet to discern it.[6]

which we must parse in the following twofold sense. First, and most basically, style is bad if it is lazy, inherited without challenge, domineering, moribund, or boring. This is, we might say, standard-issue Modernist reaction to inherited Beaux Arts classicism circa the first part of the twentieth century. The corollary denunciation is implied: if a practitioner relies on an inherited style or, worse, grows complacent in a personal range of effects like a painter or actor rendering the same basic performance, however pleasing, over and over because of audience demand, style has become the enemy of creativity.

Hence style is not banished from the lexicon so much as it is revised to split into *mere fashion*, on the one hand, and, on the other, what philosophers of mind call an *emergent property* of an age and its best creative practices. We might imagine a dynamic relationship here, between ground-level practice and high-flown rhetoric that seeks to crystallize the Zeitgeist. The latter is actually necessary for the former to flourish, even it may seem to respond as post-fact theory to ante-facto practice. Without both, and a healthy relation between them, the epoch is diminished overall. Why else, after all, would Le Corbusier have felt it necessary to issue a manifesto for the "new architecture," even though it was by all accounts an age in which manifesto was a preferred literary and political form? (Evelyn Waugh's satirical novels *Decline and Fall* (1928) and *Vile Bodies* (1930) contain some wry abuse of modernist architectural fashion—one critic judged Waugh's views "reasonably well informed and openly hostile"[7]—as well as the choice detail that one character holds a cocktail party for which the invitations are in manifesto form.[8])

I pause here to record that Rybczynski, defender of style in architecture, is no fan of fashionable jargon. He has argued that, in the void left from Modernism's collapse as the governing aesthetic in architecture, theoretical mumbo-jumbo has battled with neoclassicist revisionism for control of the profession's psych. Neither is a good solution to this void (if it really is one; I frankly doubt it); but the bafflegab of architectural theory is in any event a more obscure enemy to good, performatively ethical building. In a puckish article called "A Discourse on Emerging Tectonic Visualization and the Effects of Materiality on Praxis," he chides the profession for falling into the sorts of linguistic bogs that have lately afflicted comparative literature and the artworld.[9] *Discourse* itself is defined in this harsh anti-lexicon as "What architects talks about when they talk about architecture." *Tectonic* is glossed as "Nothing to do with geology, it signifies, so far as I understand it, anything to do with building." *Morphosis, Ennead*, and *Oculus* are identified as architecture firms in, respectively, Los Angeles, New York, and Chongqing. (That's pretentious, maybe, but it isn't jargon.)

Personally, I have no quarrel with criticism of alienating, insider-trading expert-speak. I have suffered through more than a few architecture grad-school crit sessions that were suffused with hand-waving and often inaccurate "philosophical" meanderings, usually offered more by the examiners than by the hapless candidates. Meanwhile, I have always tried to make my own philosophical writing jargon-minimal. There is *an ethical obligation* in professions to make themselves and their work understood by nonprofessionals; everything else is bullying and/or mansplaining. But we must also recall that the presumption in favor of "plain language" is itself an ideological commitment, a usually unexamined bias for the "normal" that can, as with such related notions as "realistic" and "practical," play into the hands of the current arrangement. I prefer the urgent dialectical energy of the Soixante-Huitard slogan: *Soyez realistes, demandez l'impossible* ("Be realistic, demand the impossible").

* * *

Whatever one's view on *discourse*, we stand on surer ground when it comes to the second of the two senses in which style is generally condemned, namely the adjacent kind of laziness that goes with overreliance on decoration or ornament. History records that Adolf Loos delivered the lecture "Ornament and Crime" in 1910, though it is sometimes dated to 1908. The first published version came in 1913 as "Ornament et Crime" in the French journal *Les Cahiers d'aujourdui*, then sixteen years later in original German in *Frankfurter Zeitung* as "Ornament und Verbreche." Loos's basic argument is well known; indeed, it can derived without further ado from the title of his essay alone. The influence on this anti-ornament, meaning-is-use argument is remarkable for such an apparently slight piece.[10]

In the essay, as we saw earlier, Loos makes familiar Modernist arguments against classical decoration and classical jargon: all the inherited visual and discursive vocabulary of pedimentation, column, and arch. After a visit to the United States, where he absorbed Louis Sullivan's celebrated remark that "It could only benefit us if for a time we were to abandon ornament and concentrate entirely on the erection of buildings that were finely shaped and charming in their sobriety," Loos became a dedicated foe of Art Nouveau and the Deustscher Werkbund. "The German Werkbund has set out to discover the style of our age," he said. "This is unnecessary labour. We already have the style of our age."[11]

Like Walter Gropius, Le Corbusier, and Mies van der Rohe, Loos strips his language down to sharp lines and tight corners, even as that language is used to argue, with puritanical glee, against the "decadence," "disease," "retrograde" tendencies, and even "immorality" of decorative approaches to building. Granting as locally valid the primitive impulses of children and earlier civilizations, he offers this admonishment to the modern moment: "[T]he man of our day who, in response to an inner urge, smears the walls with an erotic symbol is a criminal or a degenerate." This semi-Freudian analysis, which backlinks the Lascaux cave drawings to feces-flinging primates and children, is then pushed forward in this manner: "I have made the following discovery and pass it on to the world: *The evolution of culture is synonymous with the removal of ornament from utilitarian objects.*"[12]

It remains significant for present purposes that Loos frames his high-flown aesthetic-prophet's rhetoric in terms of *style*. "Every age had its style," he goes on, "is our age to be refused a style? By style, people meant ornament. Then I said: Weep not! See, therein lies the greatness of our age, that it is incapable of producing a new ornament. We have outgrown ornament; we have fought our way through to freedom from ornament."[13] And in this freedom is aesthetic salvation: "See, the time is nigh, fulfillment awaits us. Soon the streets of the city will glisten like white walls. Like Zion, the holy city, the capital of heaven. Then fulfillment will be come."[14]

Bracing! There is an immediate tension here, however, when these "aristocratic" Modernist blusterings, complete with Christian apocalyptic overtones, are viewed in larger historical perspective, say from mid-twentieth century on. The alleged *decadence* of decorative attachment—a charge already alive in the late nineteenth century, as Loos notes—can flow, by imperceptible but somehow inevitable links, into the reverse-pole accusations of *degenerate* aesthetics, wielded by Nazi ideologues and their lackeys. Modernist aggression against the crimes of ornament is here *flipped* into neoclassicist and fascist denunciation of the very idea of "the modern," which is subtly parsed as Jewish, elitist, and cosmopolitan in the pejorative sense. Now there is an aesthetic battle fought by rival dismissive elites, but with one—fascist Germany—in possession of weapons and institutional power as well as brushes and canvas, while the other remains weak and forever on the run.

Meanwhile, Loos's half-ironic injunction that we should set fire to towns and empires so that new, disposable furniture shall be needed and thus make work for artisans, is haunted by the actual fires of towns, books, and people that scar central Europe from 1933 to 1945. His associated facetious endorsement of planned obsolescence for domestic furnishings—the *Ikea argument*, one might anachronistically label it—is likewise tainted by the actual market failures and vast consumerist waste we have witnessed in the century or so since his essay's composition. (He could not have anticipated the *upgrade anxiety* that attends the ownership of smartphones and their various design features.)

Naturally nobody today would defend the neoclassical grandiosities of Adolf Hitler's aesthetic regime, directed in large measure by propaganda master Josef Goebbels and willing lackeys such as Leni Reifenstahl, whose *Triumph of the Will* (1935) melds neoclassical iconography with the spectacular power of film at the Nuremberg Rally of 1934, when some 700,000 Nazi soldiers and supporters gathered together to demonstrate unity after Hitler's murder of Ernst Röhm and his brownshirt Sturmabteilung (SA) paramilitary streetfighters in the so-called "Night of the Long Knives." As the critic Walter Benjamin noted, the film reduces politics aesthetics.[15] From a world-historical perspective, the rejection any such reduction counts as a victory. The 1937 "Degenerate Art" exhibition, which boldly celebrated artworks deemed unacceptable by the rising Nazi powers and sometimes removed from existing museum placement, stands as a monument of aesthetic courage under material political conditions.

But the ground-level battles were, as usual, quite bloody for individual combatants. Nor, indeed, is this war decisively over. The art historian Henry Grosshans has argued that Hitler "saw Greek and Roman art as uncontaminated by Jewish influences. Modern art was [seen as] an act of aesthetic violence by the Jews against the German spirit. Such was true to Hitler even though only Liebermann, Meidner, Freundlich, and Marc Chagall, among those who made significant contributions to the German modernist movement, were Jewish. But Hitler . . . took upon himself the responsibility of deciding who, in matters of culture, thought and acted like a Jew."[16]

Does this sound familiar in the second decade of the twenty-first century, when we might have thought the very notion was moribund? Donald Trump's notion that only neoclassical designs are suited for federal buildings, those sanctioned material structures that embody and distribute state power, lies on a straight line from the Hitlerian imperative. Both authoritarian politicians view Greek and Roman architecture as the presumptive fallback position on anything to do with state grandeur or visual exercise of impressiveness.

And, to be sure, they are not alone: when the Fifty-Third Street instantiation of the Museum of Modern Art opened in Manhattan

in 1939, its deliberatively anti-classical, street-level design (by, iron-
ically, Nazi-admiring Philip Johnson) was meant to contrast with
the intimidating stairway and imposing façade of the Metropolitan
Museum of Art uptown in Central Park. As Arthur Danto has noted,
a "Museum of Museums" would note this bold move to make art
museums less like banks and court houses—temples of finance and
law, respectively—and more like welcoming aesthetic shelters, even
or especially if the contours were straight and minimal.[17] These are,
as Danto argues, our new cathedrals—and they need not, indeed
should not, resemble the original cathedrals. (Worth noting: a *cathedral* church isn't just a magnificent one; it is so deemed because it
contains a chair from which a bishop or pope, speaking *ex cathdra*,
can invoke the doctrine of church infallibility. Power is contained
within the building, and even within the chair: the throne of reli-
gious authority.)

We noted already that the recent Trump-approved directive on neoclassical design was underwritten not by simple authority, and the
ability to exercise it, but by an aesthetic argument, however bogus.
And so now we must consider another danger word in the aesthetics
of architecture: *beauty*. This is a quality not just residing in the eye
of the beholder. It is also a cultural and political battleground. The
Trump directive, in common with those issues by Prince Charles of
the United Kingdom and other retrograde personages, supposes that
beauty means classical proportion and vocabulary. This is inherently
ridiculous, since only an aesthetic ideologue would deny that, for example, the Seagram Building, Fallingwater, or the Glass House were
beautiful. Even in the ambit of federal American buildings just in
Washington, D.C., the East Wing of the National Gallery of Art, the
Hirschorn Museum, and the Museum of the American Indian are
all demonstrably beautiful buildings in the aesthetic judgment of
at least some citizens. One can argue about the appeal of Concrete
Brutalism, but I count myself among its fans. Am I wrong? Who
says? And who says that neoclassical nonsense is *obviously* superior?

Well, Christopher Bedford, for one.[18] In an article called "Behind
the White House Move to Stop Ugly Federal Buildings (And the
Architects Who Stand in the Way," Bedford rehearses the standard

charges of anti-Modernist sentiment everywhere: the buildings are alienating, poorly constructed, unpleasing to the eye. This is the essence of the argument:

> [I]n 1901, the Department of the Treasury, which then oversaw federal architecture, issued an order that required classical architecture "for all [government] buildings as far as it was practicable to do so," adding that, "The experience of centuries has demonstrated that no form of architecture is so pleasing to the great mass of mankind as the classic, or some modified form of the classic."
>
> But then, in 1962, it was all undone by the Guiding Principles for Federal Architecture, an order that enshrined the new architectural elite's belief that it is they who rule the people and their government. "The development of an official style must be avoided," it decrees, undoing Pierre L'Enfant's careful plan for Washington. "Design must flow from the architectural profession to the government, and not vice versa."
>
> Since that day, architects, untethered from the responsibility of designing buildings that the people like to see, live in and work in, have relentlessly force-fed the public ugliness.[19]

We see here, defined in more than usually blunt language, the "blight" the citizens must endure when dealing their own state and its appurtenances. In back of the aesthetic objections lies clear resentment at the presumed cultural and intellectual *arrogance* of architects to choose their own style, and even standards of beauty, apart from those that may or may not please "the great mass of mankind" (a phrase that should strike fear into anyone's heart).

* * *

Articles like this are not hard to come by, sent into the world by writers as exalted as Tom Wolfe to journeymen toiling at lesser literary altitudes.[20] An indicative quotation from the former level: "Every child goes to school in a building that looks like a duplicating-machine replacement-parts wholesale distribution warehouse. Not even the school commissioners, who commissioned it and approved the plans, can figure out how it happened. The main thing is to try to avoid having to explain it to the parents."

On the latter elevation we find, for example, Brianna Rennix and Nathan J. Robinson offering, in the well-known aesthetic journal *Current Affairs*, an explanatory piece on "Why You Hate Contemporary Architecture (And if you don't, why you should)." Such an article writes itself, really, in trademark sophomore style one comes to know from these pieces: the overreliance on flabby adverbs ("mind-bogglingly inscrutable," "fearlessly grim," "infuriatingly un-navigable"), half- baked witticisms ("Walter Gropius, an architected whose chuckle-inducing surname belies the utter cluelessness of his designs"), and pained rhetorical protests about how critics of modernist architecture are judged by savants to be philistines. When, in reality, the writers are just holding a torch for, you know, what *everyone* recognizes as *beauty*.

And so we get this:

> The fact is, contemporary architecture gives most regular humans the heebie-jeebies. Try telling that to architects and their acolytes, though, and you'll get an earful about why your feeling is misguided, the product of some embarrassing misconception about architectural principles.

And then this:

> For about 2,000 years, everything human beings built was beautiful, or at least unobjectionable. The 20th century put a stop to this, evidenced by the fact that people often go out of their way to vacation in "historic" (read: beautiful) towns that contain as little postwar architecture as possible. But why? What actually changed? Why does there seem to be such an obvious break between the thousands of years before World War II and the postwar period? And why does this seem to hold true everywhere?[21]

My favorite part of this all-too-predictable screed was the opening flourish, which quotes the late, great Douglas Adams on the ugliness of airports: "Airports are ugly. Some are very ugly. Some attain a degree of ugliness that can only be the result of a special effort. This ugliness arises because airports are full of people who are tired, cross, and have just discovered that their luggage has landed in Murmansk (...) and the architects have on the whole tried to reflect this in their designs."[22]

That is no doubt true of *some* airports—Heathrow and O'Hare come to mind—but I wonder if Adams, before leaving the mortal plane in 2001, had the opportunity to visit Norman Foster's 1998 masterpiece in Chep Lap Kok, Hong Kong, or Paul Andreu's 1999 landmark in Shanghai Pudong, or (surely?) Eero Saarinen's enduring 1962 gem, Dulles Airport in Chantilly, Virginia, which has recently been expanded with grace. One could add architectural marvels in Singapore, Madrid, Marrakesh, Vancouver, Kuala Lumpur, Doha, Munich, Denver, and a few other places. Don't blame the airport for being an airport!

And then, as I was composing this part of our current walk, there arrived in my inbox a column by *Toronto Star* columnist Heather Mallick, whose work I mostly admire. It sported the headline "Our cities are ugly and we know who to blame." The first two paragraphs ran this way:

> Who has done the most damage to cities, the central points around which the modern world turns and the kind of interesting, intense places where most Canadians want to live? You're right, architects.
>
> They were given a free hand but now that the dull, cheap, tissue-box buildings put up after the Second World War are falling down, we have to decide what beautiful green-natured and human-friendly buildings will replace them. This time, let's not leave it to established architects from one of the most female-hostile professions extant.[23]

Even allowing for the rhetorical excesses expected of newspaper columnists, this is a silly and disingenuous piece of hackery. From the smug presumption of that "You're right," to the unsupported assertions of "free hand" and "falling down," this piece tracks the standard-nonsense amateur-critic's narrative of twentieth-century architecture's depredations with nary a hiccup, or original insight, along the way.

This kind of Modern-just-equals-bad is lazy writing but, worse, it is lazy thinking. Blaming "architects" for ugly cities is like blaming "lawyers" for human corruption. The accompanying image was of the John P. Robarts Library, a Concrete Brutalist masterpiece a stone's throw from my office, a building we used to call Fort Book. Its designers, Mathers & Haldenby in consultation with New York-based Warner, Burns, Toan & Lunde, imagined it as resembling a peacock in full tail-feather display, but I have always viewed it, especially at night and in the rain, as the aft section of the original Battlestar Galactica spacecraft (see the goofy 1978 TV series, not the Hobbesian-politics reboot, 2004 *et seq.*), plunged nose-first into the ground.

Anyway, I needn't belabor the larger point. These sad disputes are at least a century old, probably older, and will not submit to any rational solution (maybe especially in a university-press volume that takes seriously the ethical obligations of architecture). I personally find neoclassical designs on state-sponsored buildings entirely ugly, fascistic, and deliberately anti-individual, brute demonstrations of government power in architectural form. But I'm likewise certain that I would not be able to convince a dedicated neoclassicist of this view. Kant argued, in the *Critique of Judgment* (1790), that one's aesthetic judgments are intended to command agreement from others—we believe we are *right* when we judge of beauty, not simply waving our hands. But Kant also recognized that, in practice, such assent was scant.

If you have state power on your side, including especially the ability to bestow or withdraw commissions—well, that forces people to agree with you, doesn't it? Not quite Kant's idea of rational assent, by a long throw, but pretty clearly beyond argument.

* * *

Let us not become too depressed about statism in control of architectural aesthetics. There are ways and means left to the ethical practitioner of any applied art.

Consideration of materials is once more essential here, a category whereby art meets environment. As Heidegger notes in "The Origins of the Work of Art," one of the remarkable things about paint and sculpture is that they draw from the earth in order to make, or reveal, a world.[24] Pigment and canvas, marble and granite—these are elemental features of the ground beneath our feet, rendered eventually into beautiful, startling, or unsettling artifacts of human creativity. The cave paintings at Lascaux are always referenced as early human art-making precisely because they create narrative and representation on the physical surface of the earth itself, using colors drawn from that same earth.

In architecture the same principles hold with even greater force. A building must stand upon the earth. It is constructed of materials that have themselves been drawn from that same soil, albeit often with elaborate intervention by other technology. A hut is a gathering of earth, as we noted. A log cabin is the result of saw, adze, plane, and chisel. A temple will require marble cut into slabs and finished. A house needs bricks and glass, a skyscraper steel and concrete— and so on, a progression everyone knows instinctively.

Materials are not just structural, however. Interior wood is considered warm, concrete sometimes is reviled for being cold or brutal—though I note that Concrete Brutalist buildings, first celebrated and then widely despised, are enjoying a fashion comeback at the time of this writing. Indeed, concrete is an expansive case in point when it comes to the aesthetics of materials. Its structural virtues are obvious: it is affordable, durable, relatively ductile if it contains steel rebar, and so on. It insulates and bears load with reliable efficiency. But concrete isn't just one thing, it is a range of possibility. It can also be rendered with greater or lesser quality.

Consider this satirical riff by the political humourist P. J. O'Rourke, reflecting on his arrival in Communist-era Warsaw:

> Commies love concrete, but they don't know how to make it. Concrete is a mixture of cement, gravel and straw? No? Gravel, water and wood pulp? Water, potatoes and lard? The concrete runway at Warsaw's Miedzynarodowy airport is coming to pieces. From bumpy landing until bumpy take-off, you spend your time in Poland looking at bad concrete. Everything is made of it—streets, buildings, floors, walls, ceilings, roofs,

window frames, lampposts, statues, benches, plus some of the food,
I think.[25]

This riff is funny because it is at least a tiny bit true. It's not just true
of Communist countries, either. Where money is scarce and quality
materials are expensive, compromises may begin to creep in.

When I spent some staying in one of the 1,160 apartments in
Oscar Meier's São Paulo masterpiece, the Edifício Copan (1950) near
Plaça da República, I was repeatedly struck by how both the exterior
balconies and interior walls were crumbling before my eyes. The ex-
tensive external staircases, meant to facilitate movement between
apartments, appeared decidedly unsafe. The celebrated curving
design of this building, and its sloping base, negotiated a complica-
tion and pleasing footprint. But the structure itself felt like it might
tumble to the ground at any moment. It was difficult to enjoy the
spectacular skyline views from thirty stories up when the floor beneath your feet felt unstable. (Of course, in fact it was not. The tiny,
slow moving, coffin-like elevators, on the other hand, were objec-
tively scary.)

Aesthetic objections to concrete are more widespread; but as I and
many others have argued, concrete can be and often is a truly beautiful material. It is biddable, forming to virtually any shape; it is not
simply gray, as so often charged, but a whole spectrum of shades, like
a black-and-white film, especially as weather changes. Rained-upon
concrete is an unexpected aesthetic gift.[26]

Builders are seeking new, more sustainable materials as the architectural world evolves. The engineered material mass timber, for example, is proving popular with designers who want the load-bearing
elements of a building to be made of wood, and sometimes *also* want
the wood to be a primary aesthetic element. (Buildings where the
wood is an accent or grace note are not considered "mass timber
buildings.")

Fears that structures whose primary load-bearing structure is
wood arouse anxiety in some observers, because of fire hazard; but
the reality is that mass timber can often be safer than steel framing
in a fire since it is actually less likely to suffer the melt-and-collapse

tragedy of the 2001 World Trade Center attack. The wood can also then become the primary interior design feature, as the Cooper River Beech tower in Chicago, an eighty-story residential skyscraper conceptualized by the firm Perkins+Will.[27]

In my hometown of Toronto, mass-timber construction has proven extremely popular for its potential fusion of pleasing aesthetic elements and environment-friendly, renewable materials. At 77 Wade Avenue, for example (BNC Architecture and Urban Design, 2019), is an eight-story, 150,000 square foot business tower, among the tallest and largest mass-timber buildings in North America. The Arbour, part of George Brown College (Moriyama and Teshima, design 2018) is a striking, almost cathedral-like structure set to begin in 2021, aiming for net-zero carbon emissions.

One could go on. The point, I think, that the aesthetics of architecture are inextricable from the materials, and if it is not quite canonical that form follows function, no one amateur or professional can fail to appreciate a building, which is a work of art as well as a machine for living, working, or serving any subset of human desire.

Don't walk by too fast. Tarry a bit, as you would in an art museum. The great thing is, you can touch these works without being cautioned by a security guard. Tactility doesn't get you thrown out; it allows you to be drawn in.

Now: before we walk into another, even more obviously political neighborhood, let us turn our steps back from the street and toward the studio and let drift a few final aesthetic-ethical thoughts.

Philosophers of art like to say that media such as music or film are *time-based*—which is to say that these forms of creation cannot work their own peculiar magic unless the listener or viewer submits to the duration of the work, its deployment of succession. The musical score is not the work of art, nor is the bare script. We voluntarily agree to the temporal capture on which such works insist. The notion of *time-based* aesthetic media should really be revised to be *time-revealing*. We do not, indeed cannot, presume temporality beforehand; the works themselves open up the space of reflection on succession and sequence of notes or images.

Other plastic media—sculpture, painting, architecture—are not wedded to duration in the same way. They exist, as it were, all at once. To be sure, one must spend time to appreciate a sculpture or painting, and one must appreciate a building over time: entering and exiting, seeing it at various times of day, over weeks, months, even years. One obvious aesthetic dimension of architecture is its persistence. This opens up a reflective territory in which we consider that, *contra* traditional accounts, architecture is not just the ordering and manipulation of space, but also of time. After its own fashion, architecture is as time-revealing as music or film: it enables, if it does not quite enforce, an experience of succession.

How so? Well, happily or otherwise, buildings are built to last. This is a key element of their aesthetic presence in our shared consciousness, and the result of a complex aesthetic procedure. In the ordinary course of things, a studio sketch becomes a drawing, and then the drawing becomes a blueprint of plan and elevation, organized by program as well as style. Then, laboriously, the building is erected, the material result of rich aesthetic engagements. It stands for a time, perhaps a long time, and the aesthetic (and ethical) sum of the building cannot be calculated unless and until all of its effects upon generations of viewers and dwellers have been taken into account.

But we all know that many buildings that get designed never get built; and moreover that the sketch of any building, completed or not, marks its own aesthetic achievement. At high levels of architectural practice, as noted previously, especially in theory-heavy graduate schools, having an unbuilt design is a higher status-good than merely building something.[28] The sketch and the drawings, plus lately AutoCAD files and associated software, are everything when we come to judge the aesthetic integrity of a design.

Like most people interested in architecture, I have no problem with this. Sometimes, indeed, material economic conditions are a factor. Consider this analysis by *New York Times* critic Jason Farago:

In the wake of the 2008 financial crisis, architecture found itself back at the drafting table. Clients got spooked (or went broke), construction rates plummeted in the United States and Europe, and young architects in particular had to find new ways to work. And so this past decade has greeted a welter of digital projects, performances, pop-up designs and "paper architecture," by practitioners born too late for big budgets . . . These young architects are heirs to a deep tradition of architecture beyond building.[29]

The article was a celebration of the unbuilt designs of Jean-Jacques Lequeu (1757–1826), a master of gorgeous but often impracticable architecture. But the unbuilt can be, in the dynamic tensions of the ethics of aesthetic commitment, even more significant than the built.

These unrealized designs are not failures; they are visionary moments, opportunities for further inspiration. As with the design of fictional or fantastical edifices, or the imagining of maps to made-up realms, such practices engage us at once on the level of possible and actual.

In sum: not all great buildings are made of stone, brick, concrete steel, or glass. Some are made merely of paper, mind, and drafting tools. This is not so much going *beyond* architecture, as the headline on the *Times* article indicates, as it is working *back to* and *within* the heart of architecture. I mean the place where, as Schiller or Kant would say, we are motivated by the free play of imagination, ideas, and associations.

A commitment to aesthetic responsibility is, as I have been suggesting, itself an ethical commitment. To be dedicated to aesthetic norms is a form of duty, even heroism: such dedication is the mark of a true professional. At the same time, this commitment also has political and ideological implications. One's personal architectural walks may never venture beyond the drafting board or studio— and yet one is, inevitably, engaged with the world at large. And *that* is beautiful, no matter what your specific style preferences might be.

Let us remind ourselves of the orienting questions. *Who do you work for?* Clients, regulators, engineers, tenants—yes, yes. But also norms of beauty and aesthetic achievement. Everything else is just what Robert Venturi, Steven Izenour, and Denise Scott Brown called "decorated sheds."[30] There is nothing wrong with sheds, decorated or otherwise: they shelter and provide, protect and house. Nor do we need always to create "ducks," where form exactly communicates function. This would grow tiresome and, ultimately, gruesome.

Architectural art has many shades in between, whether on paper or in the surround. That is the point, and the duty.

5
Creating Justice

More than two decades ago, the Kansas City architect Bob Berkbile began to press the American Institute of Architects (AIA), the United States' largest and most powerful professional organization, to recognize the pressing urgency of sustainable buildings. The subsequent story is well known: Berkbile and others were able to convince the AIA to adopt was known, in 1989, as CPR or Critical Planet Rescue. This set of ideas, really a manifesto about environmentally responsible building design, then evolved into a central AIA committee with reach into the U.S. Environmental Protection Agency and the Bill Clinton White House, which in 1993 announced a retrofit of the nation's cherished presidential residence as a "model for efficiency and waste reduction."

A further development in 1998 and after resulted in now-familiar codes of LEED certification—Leadership in Energy and Environmental Design. LEED has four levels of certification: Certified, Silver, Gold, and Platinum. For many architects, a Platinum LEED certification is both a personal and professional goal. Not only is this responsible building practice, using sustainable materials palettes, but it is good for business: it's not simply greenwashing to offer clients and customers a structure that meets their own ideas of stepping lightly on the planet and leaving a minimal carbon footprint for future generations. Like the standards of glass that no longer invite birdstrikes in migration alleys—my own city, Toronto, is one of these, with neck-broken birds to be seen at the foot of old-glass buildings every season—this is actually easy responsible management. You don't have to be an environmental rebel

The Ethics of Architecture. Mark Kingwell, Oxford University Press (2021). © Mark Kingwell.
DOI: 10.1093/oso/9780197558546.003.0006

to work within LEED certification guidelines, or to use materials that are not toxic or actively damaging to the natural world.

But more recently it has been argued, persuasively, that LEED does not go nearly far enough. A new generation of architects, mindful of social as well as environmental costs generated by the built environment, have developed what are increasingly known as JUST certifications. The leading version of this is pioneered, as of this writing, by the International Future Living Institute. It offers a template for certification to firms of many kinds, not just in architecture, who wish to go on record as supporting diversity, equity, employee health and benefits, stewardship, and responsible supply chains for materials and subcontractors.[1] (The last is especially important, since upstream costs and damages are often apparently washed away by downstream good intentions, even when this is not in fact the case.) Once more, as of this writing, a fairly significant and growing number of organizations have signed on to JUST certification, including architects, structural engineers, construction companies, and design firms.[2]

Now of course it is easy to twit these firms for signing on to "fashionable" ideas of social justice, the kind of thing that gets people mocked by right-wing commentators as "SJW" virtue-signaling. But consider how the LEED initiative looked at its inception, an apparently "Birkenstock-and-granola" effort (as one critic put it at the time) to make the hard-edged efforts of creators and builders into a sort of hippie territory of good intentions. But LEED has a material effect on building and environments. It is a solid undertaking with real results. JUST could likewise prove the same, especially for emerging generations of designers and builders, who feel burdened with greater social awareness and a justified wariness about "great man" or "monumental" assumptions in the profession.[3]

Naturally we must ask: What, exactly, is justice in this context? My core academic training was in the subfield of political philosophy known as justice theory. This means the examination of theoretical arguments concerning the basic structure of society. *Who gets* the stuff that is there to get: opportunities, wealth, benefits, rewards, high offices, honors? And *on what basis* do they get them: Merit, birth, experience, skill, learning, popularity? These are obvious questions, which nevertheless lack obvious answers. Or, to put it somewhat better, the answers that are accepted as obvious are often pernicious or self-serving.

So we might say, paraphrasing Forrest Gump, that justice is as justice does—which is perhaps to say, we know good (i.e., politically good) architecture when we see it. But that is too pat. The task of justice *theory* is to question the apparently obvious answers and probe them for weaknesses and fallacies, including ones that may attend to blinkered thinking based in specific modes or fashions of architectural education. What we might call *just building* is an undertaking with clear and challenging limits, because political forces and human nature are everywhere involved. But for those of us who advocate it, whether we are designers, critics, or simply citizens, this notion of justice in architecture remains an essential undertaking.

On this particular walk in the woods of our subject, I won't bore you with long, theory-laden answers about all that. But I will just say a few things that might spark some future conversations. Consider the basic conditions of housing and homelessness. How is that some of the most prosperous and beautiful cities in the world still have people living without reliable shelter, even in subzero and otherwise in hospitable weather? Consider, in turn, public space. How is that apparently shared spaces are so consistently contested, as, say, between drivers, cyclists, and pedestrians? What is the distinction between public and private anyway, and is that distinction a public property or debatable space?

Down the line from all of these justice concerns, and others, lies a looming but spectral issue to which we generally give insufficient concern. I mean our justice duty to future generations. Almost all of political discourse is directed at the current time-slice of human mortality, what G. K. Chesterton memorably called "the small and arrogant oligarchy of those who merely happen to be walking about."[4] Environmental awareness and activism have changed arrogance this to some degree, not least because younger humans are schooling their elders in the damage done and what might be executed in limiting it. But justice for future generations goes well beyond this.

The notion of future justice seems to raise immediately the cognate issue of intergenerational justice. The most widely accepted version of justice to future generations is found in John Rawls's magisterial *A Theory of Justice* (1971). The basic orientation of his discussion is twofold.[5] First: in the original position, where his hypothetical social contractors don't know who, in particular, they are—including to which generation they belong—a unanimous decision will be made for the fair synchronic, as well as diachronic, distribution of goods and services. In the event, Rawls argues that this distribution will follow his two principles of justice, namely, that there will be (a) equal access to life options, and (b) a "difference" mechanism that will guarantee that the least well off will derive some benefit from any allowable social inequality. Second: the general claim that the site of justice is the "basic structure of society," to use Rawls's widely adopted phrase, seems to take sufficient account of persons both living and to come who will exist under that basic structure.

Rawls therefore argues that the original-position contractors agree on a *savings principle*, which is "subject to the further condition that they must want all previous generations to have followed it." He goes on: "Thus the correct principle is that which the members of any generation (and so all generations) would adopt as the one their generation is to follow and as the principle they would want preceding generations to have followed (and later generations to follow), no matter how far back (or forward) in time."[6] This conclusion is known as *just savings*, and while of course there can be no sense in which it is binding on factual previous generations, the principle is a part of just basic social structure because it is what the (present) contractors would have wanted from their forebears *had they been them*; and thus it is what they will (at present) bind themselves to, for the sake of those to come. The principle of just savings is therefore thought to be binding on all previous and future generations.[7]

Like much of Rawls's theory of justice, the argument is both ingenious and somehow disappointing. The disappointment is not just of the standard academic variety, whereby flaws in the argument might be discussed—though there has been plenty of that. I mean also the feeling that this conclusion, while possibly valid, seems without traction on our concrete inheritances from the past and our fraught decisions about the future. Nor does its sufficientarian logic ground a more comprehensive *trusteeship* conception of justice: the argument that we have not just a minimalist duty to leave some version of Locke's "enough and as good" to future people, but a responsibility to shift our basic position away from consumption (even curbed consumption) of goods and toward care of shared resources. I suggest that the notion of a tradition is a more viable way to plot a viable connection between the basic democratic principle (those who are affected must decide) and justice (there must be a valid distribution of resources, goods, opportunities, and potentials).

In his lively and clever book of popular Christian apologetics, *Orthodoxy* (1908), Chesterton had already addressed the issue of intergenerational injustice, using the trademark style of witty paradox. One result of this approach is that *Orthodoxy*, like Chesterton's *Heretics* (1905) before it, can be read with pleasure by believers and unbelievers alike. But his arguments are not idle or facetious, and his attacks on willful comprehensive skepticism (a fashionable disease) and rampant materialism (a form of mania) are still worth attending to. He also, perhaps unexpectedly in a book on Christian belief, has much to say about democracy, justice, and by implication the persistence of the built environment in the form of *tradition*.[8]

In the fourth chapter, called "The Ethics of Elfland," Chesterton offers this general statement: "[T]he democratic faith is this: that the most terribly important things must be left to ordinary men themselves—the mating of the sexes, the rearing of the young, the laws of the state. This is democracy."[9] (One presumes "men" might, even for him, eventually become "men and women," especially if mating and childrearing are so terribly important.) He goes on immediately, in a crucial passage:

> But there is one thing that I have never from my youth up been able to understand. I have never been able to understand where people got the idea that democracy was in some way opposed to tradition. It is obvious

that tradition is only democracy extended through time. It is trusting to a consensus of common human voices, rather than to some isolated or arbitrary record.[10]

Then, in a now-famous dilation on the point, Chesterton puts the matter in the following bold terms:

> Tradition may be defined as an extension of the franchise. Tradition means giving votes to the most obscure of all classes, our ancestors. It is the democracy of the dead. Tradition refuses to submit to the small and arrogant oligarchy of those who merely happen to be walking about. All democrats object to men being disqualified by the accident of birth; tradition objects to their being disqualified by the accident of death. . . . I, at any rate, cannot separate the two ideas of democracy and tradition; it seems evident to me that they are the same idea.[11]

These are bold claims expressed in memorable language. No wonder both *democracy of the dead* and *small and arrogant oligarchy of those who merely happen to be walking about* have passed into the lexicons of many.

There is of course much to quarrel with in Chesterton's resulting discussion of social issues. He is too forgiving of the dangers posed by doctrine, too sanguine about the mechanism of democratic franchise, and too dismissive of the idea of social change.[12] It might be thought that Chesterton emerges in this book as the answer to Kierkegaard's lamenting question: Among the Christians, is there a Christian? Yes, at least one; but he may also be the only one! Chesterton's humility and optimism are winning, but his notion of tradition is not sufficient on its face: it willfully ignores the evidence of traditions in practice, their tendencies to ossify, corrupt, and even oppress, not just on the basis of bare power or deception but *in the name of tradition itself.*

And so, despite some concluding protestations that Christian orthodoxy is "the only *logical* guardian of liberty, innovation and advance," his presumptive conception of democratic tradition is too backward-looking.[13] Guided by the idea of orthodoxy—meaning, whether Christian or otherwise, inherited ideas of right reason—such a tradition cannot take full account of the temporal dimensions of democracy. Yes, the interests of the dead, expressed in what they have left us, must indeed be part of the democratic conversation—including the conversation about democracy itself. Without an unwavering orientation in the other direction of the vector, however, we are likely to lose hold of our own duties to those who—notably, unlike the dead—have no way of expressing interests except via the exercise of our own imaginations.

It seems to me, then, that one crucial aspect of this imagination—the very same imagination that allows each of us as individuals to entertain a sense of self—must be a critical examination of the very idea of *time in its relation to justice*, and here the built environment is an essential but often overlooked dimension, the material equivalent of tradition, legacy, and future-shaping. I have been speaking, consistent with both Rawls the political philosopher and Chesterton the Christian apologist, as if time is itself uniformly distributed, typically along a more or less straight line. But we know from our own temporal existences, in which we (among other things) live out memories over and over, and attempt to construct narratives of identity by recursively imposing present knowledge on past events, that time is neither uniform nor linear.

* * *

We cannot conclude this walk without examining, briefly, perhaps the most celebrated justice-based argument about architecture in the American twentieth century. I mean the dispute between Robert Moses, arch-planner of postwar Manhattan; and Jane Jacobs, celebrant of the small and livable neighborhood.

In the 1970s this clash defined the dominant terms of urban design and planning. Moses, a grandiose and larger-than-life figure, entertained a monumental plan to transform not just Manhattan but all the five boroughs of New York City, creating public parks and swimming pools, even as he bulldozed wide swaths of old-growth urban in-fill to create expressways and large chunks of high-rise housing. The 1955 battle over a proposal to run a thoroughfare across

Washington Square Park, then as now abutted on the north side by the last stretch of Fifth Avenue, pitted him directly against Jacobs, a West Village resident and *Architectural Forum* critic with an ax to grind against any and all large-scale planning.[14] The ensuring argument, which pitted opposing philosophies of the urban as well the two central figures, is well documented.[15]

I cannot delve too deeply into this world-historical dispute here—maybe watch the opera!—but the basic contours are familiar enough. Moses was a visionary, a big-time planner; Jacobs was a resident, an opponent of what she called "Radiant Garden City" overarching design programs, a portmanteau phrase conjoining Le Corbusier's Radiant City residential development with the Garden City suburbanizing schemes of mostly English urban planners attempting to democratize single-plot comfort in mid-century sprawl. One can see merit on both sides of this debate. Moses's large-scale schemes eradicated failed neighborhoods and offered everyday solace to dwellers long denies access to grass and water, but did so at the price of heavy-handed concretization. Jacobs's plea for small-scale traditional districts and local dwelling were a welcome riposte, but the neighborhoods she championed—the West Village in Manhattan, the North End in Boston—have proven to be meccas for the super-rich and a kind of Italian-cultural theme park, respectively.

As we all know, Washington Square was saved, to be the open-air drug market and chess-prodigy haven it remains, but Moses's imprint is everywhere evident in New York. Those of us who live in Toronto, and who have also lived in the West Village (this category would embrace not just me), tend to cherish the idea that Jane Jacobs, in later life, settled on the Canadian city's Annex neighborhood, the Yoda of sustainable urban sensibility.

Moses and Jacobs get most of the attention, but the debates about North American urban planning are certainly not limited to them. Adam Gopnik, a Montreal-raised New York resident, with stops along the way in Paris, essayed a survey of the influence of Ed Logue "the long-reviled master of 'urban renewal.' "[16] Reflecting on his childhood in a subsidized Philadelphia high-rise, where his parents graduate students (both later to become professors at McGill University in Montreal), Gopnik relates a familiar lesson:

> This was the heyday of urban redevelopment, when city planners, doing what was then called "slum clearance," created high-density, low-cost public housing, often on a Corbusian model, with big towers on broad concrete plazas. In the still optimistic late fifties and early sixties, it was possible to imagine and actually use public housing as its original postwar planners had imagined it could be used: not as a life sentence but as a cheerful, clean platform that people of various racial and ethnic backgrounds without much money could use in a transition to another realm of life.
>
> It was a dream that was over almost before it began and has since been condemned by all sides: by urbanists who came to hate the uniformity of its structures and their negation of street life; by minority communities who increasingly recognized these places as artificial ghettos, without the distinctive character and variety of real neighborhoods; and by the city officials who had to police the plazas.

In short, this is a version of the standard story; but particular details are worth teasing out.

Logue and Jacobs once had an onstage debate, in which Logue needled Jacobs about her highly romantic vision of her West Village neighborhood—*he'd* been out there at 8 P.M. and hadn't seen the ballet of the street that she cooed over. (Jacobs was an instinctive Whitmanesque poet, not a data collector: you don't count the angels on the head of a small merchant.) Logue also made the serious point that the emerging anti-renewal consensus was fine for someone who already had a safe place in the West Village. For those who didn't, it was just a celebration of other people's security. [. . .] But what defeated people like Logue on the ground was the increasingly ago-nized racial politics of big cities.

And so, with replies such as these, Gopnik stands revealed as a bit of a Whitmanesque poet himself, after his somewhat self-satisfied fashion (I have no idea if he lives in the West Village, but I imagine his household security is pretty tight). These are the final lines of his essay:

> We want a generous state investment in affordable housing—which means subsidized housing—but we want it not to look like most of the affordable housing that's been built before. (It's noteworthy that the [New York mayor Bill] de Blasio administration's public-housing initiatives tend to involve rehab more than construction.) We want Logue's principles and Jacobs's places. We want the project of public housing so long as what we build does not look like a public-housing project. The contradictions are self-evident, but, then, cities are contradictions with street lights, or else they are not cities at all.

Well, sure; but that little rhetorical *do-si-do* is not much to go on if you are actually designing buildings for real cities.

Architects are not urban planners. But the ethics of the profession once more press on the central question: *Who do you work for?* I think many of us would like simply to believe it is *the city as such*, the built environment, the conurbation and its residents. But life is rarely simple, and builders never work alone.

In order to understand our shifts of time-sense in leisure, or anyway this idealized notion of leisure, let us consider how time works when it comes to the realms of human existence.

In his brisk history of secular political consciousness and the public sphere, *Modern Social Imaginaries*, Charles Taylor remarks in passing how different concepts of time, or time-consciousness, are necessary for the emergent modern political order. "The eighteenth-century public sphere thus represents an instance of a new kind: a metatopical common space and common agency without an action-transcendent constitution, an agency grounded purely in its own common actions."[17] This "metatopical common space" was, crucially, continuous and evenly distributed across its participants; that is why it could become the basis for what we now recognize as democratic civil society.

Despite this continuity and equality, however, it was not considered to have originated *ex nihilo*: there are founding myths and moments that are considered to create the possibilities of public space. But these moments of origin, Taylor argues, "are displaced onto a higher plane, into a heroic time, an *illud tempus* which is not seen as qualitatively on a level with what we do today." And so, "[t]he founding action is not like our action, not just an earlier similar act whose precipitate structures ours. It is not just earlier, but in another kind of time, an exemplary time."[18]

The distinction Taylor suggests here has many forebears. One clear way of capturing its impact hinges on the fact that Greek has two words that both translate as "time": *chronos* and *kairos*. Chronological time is the time of measurement and portioning, the time that passes. In its modern manifestation, the history of chronological time is nicely traced by both Taylor and other, more radical thinkers such as Guy Debord, in *Society of the Spectacle* (1967). This conception of time is crucial to the emergence of a shared public sphere—but also to the emergence of a work-world in which time can be subject to transaction. This is especially true in the special set of social relations that Debord calls "the spectacle," in which everything and everyone is a commodity. This is secular time, in the sense that it is "of the age": the space of everydayness, work, and exchange.

The visible sign of this time, as Lewis Mumford among others has noted, is of course the clock. The mechanism of keeping good time, once the holy grail of sailors looking to measure longitude, is here revealed as the enabling condition of capitalist labor relations. "The popularization of time-keeping," Mumford notes, "which followed the production of the cheap standardized watch, first in Geneva, was essential to a well-articulated system of transportation and production."[19] The clock keeps time by making its units identical and measured; it appears first as a shared community property in (as it might be) the town hall or church tower, matching the more ancient tolling of bells to a visual representation of time passing.

Later, as technology advances, the mechanism of *chronos* time is bionically conjoined to the human frame in the form of the pocket watch and, eventually, the wristwatch. When I fasten on a wristwatch, in other words, I am signaling to myself and others my contract with the telling of time, expressing an agreement in some sense with the proposition that time is money. The same integration of technology and biology is essential to the logic of time-and-motion studies in factory production, as exemplified by the "scientific over-sight" model of Frederick Winslow Taylor. "The enormous saving of time," Taylor writes in *The Principles of Scientific Management* (1911), "and therefore increase in the output which it is possible to effect through eliminating unnecessary motions and substituting fast for slow and inefficient motions for the men working in any of our trades can be fully realized only . . . from a thorough motion and time study, made by a competent man."[20]

We can summarize the qualities of secular, chronos time this way: it is (i) everyday, (ii) profane, (iii) homogeneous, (iv) linear, (v) horizontal, and (vi) egalitarian. We constantly encounter this time, measuring it and meeting its demands by being on time, matching our movements and achievements to its punctums, saving time and spending time, each of us equally available to time, and having it available to us. Debord closely associates this time with the emergence of labor mechanisms and the bourgeois conception of society, taking time away from the more natural cyclical rhythms of seasonal agriculture and, before it, hunting-gathering to create a time-world in which production is potentially constant. Workers may now punch in to the line *twenty-four-seven*, as we would now say, making the relation to the time-clock explicit. Consistent with orthodox Marxist critique, Debord argues that this process is insep-arable from the emergence of class, and so class conflict.

In a crucial middle section of *Society of the Spectacle*, "Time and History," Debord notes how time itself becomes a form of social dis-tinction and conflict in the course of this triumph of *chronos* time:

> The social appropriation of time, the production of man by human la-bour, develops within a society divided into classes. The power which constituted itself above the penury of the society of cyclical time, the class which organizes the social labour and appropriates the limited sur-plus value, simultaneously appropriates the *temporal surplus value* of its organization of social time: it possesses for itself alone the irreversible time of the living. The wealth that can be concentrated in the realm of

power and materially used up in sumptuous feasts is also used up as a squandering of *historical time at the surface of society*.[21]

Once measured and parceled out, subjected to transaction in the form of paid labor, time immediately becomes a commodity with the potential, like any commodity, to support an upper-tier, luxury version of itself. Free time, leisure time, ample time, time off—these all immediately beckon as goods at the margins of a world ruled by time-as-labor and labor-as-time.

It is not necessary to detail here how the commodification of time creates the familiar pathologies of demented leisure characteristic of late capitalism: the living-for-the-weekend enthrallment that, with every reference to "hump day" or "TGIF" party emphasizes the unshakable dominance of the work week.[22] Too often concealed is the persistence and bravery of those workers who demanded the regulated ten-hour, and eventually eight-hour, workday, and still later the two-day weekend.[23] Of more immediate interest, though, is the fact that those battles about time already accepted the premise of what time was. Both Taylor and Debord note that this secular, *chronos* time of labor and production-consumption achieves— one might even say *must* achieve—global reach. It is part of what Heidegger calls "the age of the world picture," the picture in which everything, including ourselves and our temporality, are in principle available for disposal: the comprehensive *standing reserve* or *enframing* (*Ge-stell*) of technology whereby everything, including human desire and possibility, is made fungible in the name of use.[24]

Debord joins other Marxist critics such as E. P. Thompson in noting the effects of this time: "With the development of capitalism, irreversible time is *unified on a world scale*. Universal history becomes a reality because the entire world is gathered under the development of this time. . . . What appears the world over as *the same day* is the time of economic production cut up into equal abstract fragments. Unified irreversible time is the time of the *world market* and, as a corollary, of the world spectacle."[25]

Thompson: "Indeed, a general diffusion of clocks and watches is occurring (as one would expect) at the exact moment when the industrial revolution demanded a great synchronization of labour." Thus a new ethos of punctuality and efficiency is born: "In all these ways—by the division of labour; the supervision of labour; fines; bells and clocks; money incentives; preaching and schooling; the suppression of fairs and sports—new labour habits were formed and a new time discipline was imposed."[26]

And compare Charles Taylor: "A purely secular time-understanding allows us to imagine society horizontally, untouched by any 'high points,' where the ordinary sequence of events touches higher time, and therefore without recognizing any privileged persons or agencies, such as priests and kings, who stand and mediate at such alleged points. This radical horizontality is precisely what is implied in the direct-access society, where each member is 'immediate to the whole.'"[27]

Now, Taylor may be thought too sanguine about this larger temporal development in modernity, even though he does allow that there are persistent local verticalities even in the comprehensively horizontal world of the secular: uneven access to goods, disjointed proximity to glamor or celebrity, corruptions of power. But Debord's sense of the dominance of spectacle in a society in which cyclical time has been lost, while accurate enough, may seem to invite a kind of nostalgia or romanticism about the time out of time. One may accept the value of Debordian Situationism's tactics of *dérive* and *détournement*—drifting and repurposing through the byways of the spectacle-dominated city, rather than resisting in some pre-doomed alternative organization—but still detect an odor of charming failure in the analysis.

* * *

The larger point about both the benefits and the costs of secular time is politically significant. Even as it invited commodification and disposal, the achievement of egalitarian secular time was a necessary condition for the emergence of popular sovereignty in full force. Without a sense of immediate access to a non-hierarchical present, however attenuated or subject to doubt, there can be no conviction that we, the people, are the creators of our social order, nor that, to use Taylor's words, popular elections—not bloodlines, transcendental access, or historical precedent—are "the only source of legitimate power." He goes on: "But what has to take place for this change to come off is a transformed social imaginary, in which the idea of foundation is taken out of the mythical early time and seen as something that people can do today. In other words, it becomes something that can be brought about by collective action in contemporary, purely secular time."[28]

This cannot be done purely through action at the level of secular time, however. Not only will a *narrative of origin* continue to prove necessary to the development of publicly open democratic society, it will also be necessary to keep open the ever-present possibility of an *eruption of justificatory argument* concerning legitimacy. This kind of argument is distinct from the day-to-day business of collective action, still more from the policy making and regulatory business-as-usual of politics.

The narrative of origin is familiarly sketched in the various versions of contractarian thought experiment that come down to us in the liberal tradition: Hobbes's state of nature, Locke's pre-social order, even Rawls's original position—though the last does not indulge in a dubious appeal to history or human nature that undermines our respect for the early modern examples. Rousseau, notably, who sounded such a strong keynote in *The Social Contract* about man being born free but living everywhere in chains, would chide Hobbes for not stripping away enough of the accretions of social contagion in his conception of natural man. The humans for whom pre-social existence was solitary, poor, nasty, brutish, and short, were, Rousseau argued, already highly socialized beings trained to pursue their own competitive self-interest. This criticism, though well aimed, does not, however, thereby lend more credence to Rousseau's alternative, which invites the parallel objection that it is a species of special pleading. Rawls's atemporal version of a justificatory scheme, with the original position framed as a thought experiment that one might undertake at any time, draws fire concerning what, precisely, must be excluded by the veil of ignorance in order to generate a unanimous outcome. The political narrative of origin will always be controversial.

The eruption of justificatory argument, because it is grounded in actual rather than imagined history, seems more promising. Such an eruption might be discerned in historical narratives of the public-democratic process, such as Bruce Ackerman's magisterial account of the American republic, in which the Founding plays the originary role, including sometimes heated appeals to the Founders' intentions, but open to returns to that baseline discourse at times of crisis: the Reconstruction after the Civil War, the New Deal in the wake of the Depression. Ackerman argues that the truly democratic republic, no matter how atavistic its self-narrative, can never foreclose on the option of returning to the discursive drawing board.[29] To be sure, Founders' Intent remains itself a disputed property, both in everyday judicial argument and in returns to constitutional first principles. More darkly, the same return to basic legal framing can be glimpsed in Carl Schmitt's notion of the *exception*, that which is decided upon by the sovereign; and in Walter Benjamin's rejoinder about the *violence* in all acts of political establishment.

The contrastive term for secular time gives us an insight about what this complicated narrative of origin and legitimation might look like: the tradition that is distinctively public and democratic. That is, we are now in a position to characterize the useful diacritical opposite of *chronos* time, namely *kairos* or transcendental time. It is (i) mysterious, (ii) divine, (iii) eternal, (iv) infinite, (v) vertical, and (vi) hierarchical. In many cases, of course, precisely this kind of time—the time of divine intervention or communion with the eternal realm—is familiar as part of an antidemocratic social order, in which privileged access, or anyway claims thereto, keeps a steeply hierarchical class division firmly in place, ostensibly as part of a Great Chain of Being or Divine Universal Scheme.

The forerunner here might be, of course, the Platonic Theory of the Forms, with realms of knowledge and reality arranged in rigid order. The upward ascent of the self-freed slave of Plato's Cave, struggling through blindness and pain toward the sun's light, is an ascent to eternity as well as reality—for they are one and the same.

But these towering religio-philosophical edifices have their less grandiose analogs even in our own world. I mean, for example, the sense of time beyond time that still marks genuine leisure, play, and idleness, the *skholé* of Aristotle even now to be found in our aimless games and blissful moments of "flow"; or the true holiday, where the usual tyranny of work and use-value is suspended in the name of carnival or sabbath. The common desire for what the Germans call *Freizeit*—time free of obligation—is united with the transcendence of time available to almost any North American urban dweller in a baseball game, say, where time is told only in outs and innings, in a pastime that is played in what is usually called a park. (The cognate game of cricket arguably offers even more in the way of time out of time!)

In his paean to baseball, Milton scholar and commissioner of baseball A. Bartlett Giamatti references *Paradise Lost* (IV, 434–45) in an expression of Aristotelian leisure, which he calls "the ideal to which our play aspires." From the poem: *Free leave so large to all things else, and choice/Unlimited of manifold delights.* "But in fact, the serpent is already there," Giamatti notes, "and our sports do not simulate, therefore, a constant state. Rather, between days of work, sports or games only repeat and repeat our efforts to go back, back to a freedom we cannot recall, save as a moment of play in some garden now lost."[30]

These and other *ludic episodes* to be found within everyday existence are portals to the gift of public space, for they remind us of the resistance to transactional reduction that grounds the most valuable features of our common life. But they are also, as we have seen, high-risk propositions in an age of terror.

And here danger lurks. This is not the danger of an external natural world, whose savage indifference prompted our building in the first place; it is instead the danger within—human-caused violence, worse than indifferent even when its motives are unclear and unleashed on an innocent public. We shoulder these risks every time we leave the safety, however illusory, of the private space. In economic terms, we balance off the positive externalities of public space (stimulation, cultural opportunity, perhaps new relationships) against the negative externalities created by the very same material forms (crime, harassment, rudeness, violence). Every traversal of a threshold, performed however unconsciously, strikes a new bargain with time and terror.

Thresholds serve as liminal alteration sites, neither inside nor outside but establishing the demarcation thereof. Traditionally, the "thresh" was fresh hay or grass, placed in the doorway to offer a cleansing opportunity—we wipe our shoes or boots before entering the interior from the dirty outside. The metaphorical extension is then obvious: over a threshold we move from the profane to the sacred, from the public to the private, from the world of commerce and exchange to the protected space of domestic activity. Typical interiors are temples, hearths, or bedrooms, offering warmth and sustenance both material and spiritual.

Importantly, the distinction between public and private space is itself a public achievement: an agreement, either in principle or by long practice, of what will be excluded from community view and even, in some cases, from the reach of the law. If the threshold were not so publicly agreed, the fragile balance of these realms of human existence would not hold. I may lock my doors at night to enclose the private realm, but if there is no punishment for those who breach the lock, there is in effect no lock. There must be at least some measure of consensus on where the public leaves off and the private begins— and vice versa—so that each may thrive. The very idea of public space is predicated on the Aristotelian-Arendtian notion that *action* takes place in public, however much it relies on private resources and preparation. We may repair to the home to recuperate, regroup, rethink; but a sustained retreat from public life is, many of us believe, antithetical to community and even justice.

In the current context, then, two problems immediately arise that are distinct from a more familiar third, what I will call The Standard Problem. The Standard Problem of public space has been understood to be one of limits on access to such space. That is, given what we know about controlled resources and the depredations of capital markets on all aspects of human life, how can we *open up* public spaces to make them more inclusive, diverse, and universally available? The logic of The Standard Problem is, as mentioned, that public spaces should ideally be public goods: non-rival (nobody's enjoyment of them impairs anyone else's) and non-excludable (nobody can be denied access). One way of summarizing The Standard Problem is to reference Lefebvre's celebrated "right to the city." We desire cities that are open in (at least) the sense that their public spaces should be available to everyone who wishes to enjoy them, with no countervailing costs to others who likewise wish to do so.

The two new problems subvert the basic logic of The Standard Problem, and they are thus the two related prongs of the new terrorism of time in public spaces. The first is perhaps the more obvious: what we may call *defections* or *buy-outs* from public space.[31] By these terms I mean systematic retreats from public spaces that have become a common luxury good in the age of postmodern capitalism. Those with the relevant resources can choose to live their lives almost entirely in private, disdaining both the noise and bustle of public spaces and the injunction that action—political life as such—can only be enacted publicly. Such people are really no longer citizens of a democratic polity; they exist on a transnational plane where taxes, say, when they cannot be avoided altogether, are regarded as tolerable fines on the margins of their freedom.

Defections and buy-outs are distinction modalities of this public-space problem. The typical defection involves a retreat behind barriers both real and notional: gated communities and elaborate home security, but also velvet ropes, first-class lounges, and the strange nonexistence of owning multiple homes (Manhattan, Hamptons, Miami, Aspen is the current "Four-Pack" dream). When someone may be anywhere, he is essentially nowhere. Small-time defections are also possible, however, as when we spend more and more time online, watching Netflix, playing video games, or dallying with social media. Every retreat from public space in favor of the cosseted private realm is a small blow against democratic politics—once more, at least on this idealized model.

Buy-outs are more explicit, running a gamut from the silly (paying someone to wait in line for a seat on a roller coaster or at a theater premiere) to the comprehensive (using accumulated capital to influence politics well beyond legal one-vote personhood[32]). A totalized combination of defection and buy-out might be exemplified by a

Silicon Valley figure such as Peter Thiel, who has used accumulated wealth to opt out of democratic politics altogether, viewing them as antithetical to his goals of "innovation" and "disruption." Even those multibillionaires who donate portions of their wealth to high-profile charities are playing a private game that represents a more nuanced buy-out of publicness. When I put my vast wealth in the service of specific causes, I act to hollow out of the general principle of the public as such.

The second problem is harder to grasp, since its contours are necessarily hazy. But with it, we return to our starting point: the terrorism of time in public spaces. Because the second problem is the matter of risk in public. There is, after all, good reasons for defections on a limited-rationality calculation. Bad things can happen when I expose myself to the uncertainties and negative externalities of public space. These risks once more may run from the trivial (being confronted by people I find strange on the sidewalk or in the subway) to the mortally serious (being struck down by a madman while taking my easy lunchtime stroll). The temporal element here should be obvious: the longer I spend in public, the longer I expose myself to the myriad risks that lurk there.

A tension is thus set in motion between separate demands of time. On the one hand, leisure suggests that we should enjoy public spaces in a manner that lets go of chronological time, where time is present only in the passing scene and my enjoyment of it. Our literally slower pace is a mark of this different relation to temporality. On the other hand, awareness of risk arouses a fight-or-flight reaction in our brains such that we may feel a desire to scuttle, combat-style, from place to place.

Open spaces, intended to be appreciated for their lack of building—parks, plazas, squares—are transformed into danger zones with inadequate cover, imagined snipers on every surrounding rooftop, and open roadways that invite rampaging vehicles. The video game that we left inside in order to explore the outside has somehow reached out and colonized the space, pulling us inside the game, unwilling first-person shooters who don't know how to level up.

This is a dark fantasy, to be sure, but it is sufficiently real, given recent events, to make us rethink our devotion to the right to the city. We might now speak, instead, of the *precarity of the city*. The urban death-maze imagery is inseparable from all the positive externalities that bring us into public spaces in the first place. It is not possible to render the site of leisure entirely immune to the threat of violence, for any measures that sought to do so would, at some point, tip the project into self-defeat. The public space would be destroyed, converted into yet another bunker or zip-wire enclosure, when its permeability is precisely the virtue that makes for genuine publicness.

And so what to do? Defections and buy-outs will not resolve the issue of terror, only exacerbate it, since we know that the safety they vouchsafe is itself precarious even as they hollow out existing public spaces. And all the while, some version of The Standard Problem still holds: we should always wish for, and work for, greater access to public spaces for everyone. But just as we cannot solve the problem of terrorism generally with conventional tactics, so we cannot hope to solve it in respect of public spaces with standard wishes.

In other words, the proper response to terrorism is the simple, if dangerous, one we have heard all too often: we must carry on as before, or the terrorists (of all kinds) win again. Time will carry all of us away eventually. There is no avoiding this. Nor is there any avoiding risk in life, for neither buildings nor space between buildings offer anything except temporary shelter, and solace. This is as it must be.

6

Creating Being

In our final stroll together, let us grow reflective, existential, even spiritual—but with all the ethical and political heft of previous walks along for the ride.

Some familiar studies of architecture and its phenomenology—Karsten Harries, following Gaston Bachelard, is prominent—examine the "terror of time" embodied in built forms. In addition to setting off places from space at large, these arguments suggest, architecture likewise attempts to negotiate our temporal existence through, among other things, the creation of durability. In fact, though, such attempts to control time inevitably succumb to pressures of desolation even as they, sometimes, offer transcendental *kairotic* release from the linear, chronological time of modernity. Here Guy Debord, Lewis Mumford, and others provide the requisite intellectual heft.[1] Time is not just an arrow in the metaphorical sense of being unidirectional; it is also an arrow designed to pierce the hearts and minds of all so mortal beings can know its trajectory—though never its precise striking point.

In this contribution I propose to do two things: first, to extend this argument by situating the idea of public space in this same "terror of time" logic of place, beginning with the most basic of private buildings, the hut; and second, to raise the specter of actual terrorism—parasitic violence that is sometimes perversely enabled by public space. We might think here of the brutal infliction of murder using trucks or cars in public parks or promenades. How does the potential for real violence affect our sense of time as we emerge from the fragile safety of the private building in order to enter, occupy, and enjoy public spaces? These are spaces that, unlike

The Ethics of Architecture. Mark Kingwell, Oxford University Press (2021). © Mark Kingwell.
DOI: 10.1093/oso/9780197558546.003.0007

some buildings, can never fully exclude themselves from outside penetration; their potential for terror is, we might uncomfortably acknowledge, perpetual.

When we speak *of* time we also, necessarily, speak *in* time, casting bottled messages into uncertain futures. The past overcomes every present, it is said; but the future equally overcomes every past. Since I wrote the two paragraphs above, some things had happened and others had not yet. A terrorist had, on July 14, 2016, used a rented truck to wreak havoc in the French city of Nice. The 19-ton cargo van was used by Mohamed Lahouaiej-Bouhlel to kill 86 people and injure 458 others who were celebrating Bastille Day on the Promenade des Anglais in the seaside city. This was not the first time, or the last, in which a man on a self-imagined mission weaponized a utilitarian vehicle. Not quite two years later, a deranged young man called Alek Minassian used a rented panel van to fell ten people and injure dozens more in an apparently unmotivated attack in the suburb of my city, Toronto, known as North York. His motives were terroristic in the broad sense—that is, he wanted to inspire fear—but not necessarily political. The nearest we can say is that he may have been motivated by sexual resentment and the sense of murderous anger fomented by the so-called incel (involuntary celibate) community of male online saddies who can't get a date.[2]

There have been dozens of attacks of various kinds carried out over recent years with rented trucks or vans, and police in every jurisdiction acknowledge that they are almost impossible to stop. The Nice attack, with its large vehicle and appalling body count, is still at the high threshold, but police services around the world report that this style of action is both frequent and deadly. One can easily see why: renting a truck is not procedurally difficult, and requires few legal documents, let alone a security check; driving into populated areas, often recreational public spaces, is not controlled; and once the attack begins, especially since the perpetrator has no regard for his own life, the damage in human life is likely to be high. One can kill more people more efficiently with an automatic rifle, to be sure; but for sheer convenience and ease of execution, a person bent on killing can't really beat a rental van.

Is this any different from other forms of depredation in our public spaces? I think it is, because the very innocuousness of the weapon is the new distinguishing feature. Pedestrian and cyclists are used to calling out motor vehicles as mechanisms of destruction both direct and indirect; the truck or van as murder weapon is just the logical extension of the argument. A pedestrian literally *has no chance* when a murderous, and not merely careless or stupid, driver decides to target them. One might recall here, in morbid register, the cheesy Roger Corman dystopian science-fiction film *Death Race 2000* (1975), in which a cross-country road rally is enlivened by side bets on how many people a given driver manages to run over, with extra points for brutality and targets (old people, picnicking families with young children, etc.).

The serious point from this combination of real-life and speculative sources is the nature of public space, especially when that space must for the foreseeable future accept an admixture of humans and vehicles, freedom and enforcement. Between real-life terrorism and fictional visions of spectacular evil entertainment lies the question of whether we can enjoy public spaces in the ways our theoretical forebears imagined. For myself, I have asked before in talks and papers *whether public space is a public good*. This is no idle inquiry. A public good, on basic economic understanding, is a good that is non-rival and non-excludable. That means that its routine enjoyment by me should not prevent the same enjoyment by you, or by anyone else so inclined; also that there should be no barriers in principle on who may even attempt to enjoy the good. Fresh air is a genuine public good, or should be, bordered by the usual caveats concerning pollution and pathogens. So are regulated spaces such as municipal parks and cemeteries. Even here there are of course limits: in the park near my house, families routinely use open-air grills to make a communal dinner, even though this may be close to flouting city ordinances; and dog owners walking their pets between the headstones don't always stoop and scoop, a clear violation. Nevertheless, each of them believes they are enjoying public spaces in a non-rival, non-excludable manner.

But what about the more controversial spaces of our built environment, the squares and plazas of a dense downtown? These, after all, are frames both for architecture and for the destruction of human tissue that passes for political expression by the evil ones among us, whatever their specific motives. To reveal the special challenges of public space and time we must go back to basics.

In his now-classic essay, "Building and the Terror of Time," philosopher and critic Karsten Harries offers a subtle account of the relationship between the enclosures and edifices of human construction and the underlying anxieties that both prompt such construction and render it forever unstable. The most obvious and atavistic motive for building is the creation of material safety in a world of hostile outside forces. The origin of building is The Fall itself.

"Building has been understood to be a domestication of space," Harries argues. "To domesticate space is to tame it, to construct boundaries that wrest place from space. Such constriction receives its measure from our need to control the environment. [. . .] Every house may be considered an attempted recovery of some paradise."[3] From the start, then, the project of building is intimately tied to our needs and fears. The most basic of these may be counted as the fear of death, the certainty of which is known to us but which must be kept at bay, at least temporarily, so that we may live and achieve.

As in Hobbes's transition from a state of nature where life is "solitary, poor, nasty, brutish, and short" to a stable sovereign condition, there can be no possibility of commerce, art, literature, or anything else we associate with human civilization *unless and until* there is relative freedom from death's dominion. Building is indeed essential here: we *buy time* with our structures, so that we may exploit the possibilities of a mortal span whose precise length is unknown to us. And yet, all such temporal purchases are ultimately revealed as high-interest loans from the toughest lender there is, time itself. "Thus, if we can speak of architecture as a defense against the terror of space," Harries suggests, "we must also recognize that from the very beginning it has provided defense against the terror of time."[4]

And this is true for any "building," from the most primitive huts and to the complex megaprojects of supermodernity. As Harries notes, citing an uncompleted Kafka story, "Der Bau," all creatures attempt to create a shelter of some kind, to find safety in structure. In German, *Bau* can mean both building and burrow, and we are reminded, as in Heidegger's etymological investigation of *bauen*, how primordial is the task of building. "Unable to possess the world, [the creature] tries to withdraw into its artificial environment," Harries notes. "It intends to replace nature with artful construction. But the threatening outside cannot be eliminated."[5] To see this point more clearly, let us consider a very basic structure and its relation to time: the hut.

* * *

What, after all, is a *hut*? The etymological trail suggests it is not just the idea of shelter, but the intimation of hiding—a hut conceals and covers, and its somewhat tortuous entry into the great assimilative maw of English usage was via military pragmatics. A hut, in French or German, might mean a cottage or some similar abode of retreat and respite. For the earliest English users of the imported monosyllable, it represented shelter and camouflage. Deep in the Old English linguistic roots, *hut* and *hide* are linguistic cousins.

Since then, huts have ramified their connotations across a range of meaning. Quonset huts, those half-tube prefab structures of corrugated iron and simple doors, still have a place in the military lexicon. These iconic structures, we find, acquired their name from the Quonset Point Naval Air Station in Rhode Island, where in 1941 they were first fashioned. Quonset Point in its turn was named for an Algonquian marker, a word that means "small, long place." So now point meets hut, because a Quonset hut really is a sort of portable longhouse, a government-issued chunk of basic storage or community shelter.

In anthropological terms, a hut ranks somewhere between a temporary shelter such as a tent or lean-to, on the one hand; and a more permanent structure in the form of a house or a barracks, on the other. Huts are primitive and opportunistic—they take advantage of available materials in whatever form they can be found. Mud, stones, sticks, branches, hides, or cloth might be deployed in the creation of a hut. In childhood fantasies, a discarded cardboard box was ample material for a hut, or hay bales in a barn, or boards and nails hoisted into the crux of a tree. What is a treehouse except an elevated hut, a place where we can ban outsiders, hoard comic books, and drink warm soda while scanning the field of fire?

Some huts are purely defensive, or offer platforms for ballistic re-taliation. The difference between a hut and a fort is, perhaps, only a matter of relative stability. A hut can be equally a place of solitude and refuge or a gathering of the like-minded, a communion stage. A hut can likewise be a place of pure recreation: a poolside cabana, an interlacing of palm trees next to the ocean, a miniature cabin hard by the cool waters of a mountain lake. Here, the hut offers a combination of contemplative vantage point—look at the beautiful water—and green room, possibly with accompanying drinks, for forays outside.

The landmark study of huts in their primitive form is D. C. Beard's *Shelters, Shacks, and Shanties* (1914), billed as "the classic guide to building wilderness shelters." In this comprehensive illustrated guidebook of temporary housing, much thumbed by zealous Scouts, modern-day Robinson Crusoes, and unhinged survivalists, we find every sort of structure fashioned from the world around us. Beard himself was a cofounder of the Boy Scouts of America, but he prob-ably didn't anticipate that his book would inspire off-gridders like the Unabomber or the eccentric Thomas Johnson, "the Nantucket hermit."

Johnson lived in a series of self-built underground shelters across New England—and even Hawaii—during two decades of Thoreavian reflection. "This is my church. This is my factory. This is my school," Johnson said in a television interview. "It's more than an experiment. It's an adventure in lifestyle. It's a rebel creation." But Johnson did not view himself as weird or unbalanced. "I wouldn't consider myself a survivalist, or a survival nut, but I am a survivor," Johnson said. "I consider myself a fort builder. That's something I never grew out of." In his underground hut-fort—a space that was in fact quite luxurious—he could, he said, "hear the heartbeat of the island."[6]

The most basic form of hut might be the dugout, really no more than a hole with some simple cover added. This is the human form finding its baseline shelter and cover in the earth itself. In military use, its advantages are obvious. Less dramatically, baseball teams still take shelter in dugouts when they are not fielding, a reminder that the most abstract of team games is also the most chthonic. The sun is blocked so there is shade; there is likewise camaraderie, rest, bubblegum, water, and chewing tobacco there. The necessary equipment of the contest—bats, gloves, bits of body armor—all stands ready for use in the game. This dugout is not so much a hiding place as a staging ground.

And so there is likewise a long tradition of the hut as a built feature of the great pursuits for *chasse et peche*. Hunting and fishing have long featured the hut as an element of the day in field and stream. A hunting hut holds provisions and ammunition, perhaps a necessary source of warmth and sustenance. A fishing hut will have a cleaning station, say, for the careful dressing of a fresh catch before taking it triumphantly to a kitchen or grill.

The hut is where tall tales are exchanged, memories evoked, smokes set alight, and hip flasks opened for judicious—or not so judicious—swigs of hard liquor. When we venture out to the field or fire or the rushing river, the hut grounds and orients us, it is the point of origin and return, a compass of our adventure. Even in the most luxurious of settings, where the "hut" might be a fancy lodge-like building with hot and cold running water and other lavish amenities, its basic function is not material comfort but direction.

It is home plate, ground zero, the celebrated locus known as *fons et origo*. We leave it with the high expectation of return, we hope of a triumphant tenor. The angler and hunter, it is said, are the only walkers who are happy to make their inbound journey more laden than the outbound. Weight is success, and food—even if, these days, most conscientious anglers favor the norm of catch and release (with a smartphone photo taken to mark the solitary successes).

The hut is at once utilitarian and, somehow, stranded in an odd region of the necessary and the unnecessary. That is to say, if a more temporary shelter is all we really need, why construct the hut? Surely a tent or even a humble groundsheet will do to ward off the depredations of climate and enemy? If, by contrast, we need a more permanent lodging, isn't it just practical to invest a little more time and energy and construct a house or garrison? But the special contours of what we might call "the hut-world" remains essential here, and provides a clue to the profound appeal of the hut as a structure. So let me attempt to place the hut in its deeper philosophical geography.

Martin Heidegger remains perhaps the most famous hut-dweller in the Western tradition of philosophy. Like Ludwig Wittgenstein, the Austrian genius with decidedly different philosophical proclivities, Heidegger found solace, and the opportunity to think deeply, in a rough woodside structure. Wittgenstein's favorite location was Norway; for Heidegger, the philosopher of *Blut und Boden*, it was inevitably the *Schwarzwald*—the Black Forest. Where once had disported the characters from the Brothers Grimm, Heidegger now made his own off-grid retreat. In the 1930s and after, this densely treed and mountainous region provided the philosopher with a magical home.

The hut was situated on a hillside near Todtnauberg. The basic structure is a small foursquare log house, its most arresting feature a long roof that extends back and joins the building organically to the sloping hill. The hut is rooted in place, a material illustration of the later Heidegger's notion of building (*Bauen*), explored most completely in an essay called "Building Dwelling Thinking" (1951).[7] According to the dense poetic idiom of Heidegger's work, much-quoted by architectural theorists, conventional notions of building as mere structural achievement fail to heed the linguistic "call" embedded in the verb-form of *bauen*. Most importantly, the notion of *building* also embraces *dwelling*—being at home, in place—and *cherishing* or *preserving* the world.

To build, therefore, is to engage the prospect of dwelling, which in turn is a preserving or holding. Here, and only here, is thinking made possible: the true thinking of our essence, which is the fact of *being here*.

The second major theme of this essential essay, equally relevant to the question of the hut, is Heidegger's notion of *the fourfold*.

This is often considered mystical in tone, but let us be more pragmatic: as is well known, the fourfold is a matrix of meaning that consists of (a) earth, (b) sky, (c) mortals, and (d) divinities. A genuine building—one which makes dwelling and thinking possible, or rather recognizes these as the logically necessary prior ends of building—gathers the fourfold unto itself. One needn't be a mystic or even a believer to acknowledge the force of "divinity" here. The divinities in question are the household gods or inhabiting spirits that extend across our mortal range.

Thus, a hut like Heidegger's own gathers the fourfold by sitting on the earth, by being situated under the sky. The mortals who dwell there, Heidegger and his wife Elfride, sporting their traditional costumes and drawing water or chopping wood, commune with divine presences that are more immanent than transcendent. The hut is "merely" material in its component parts, but as a building that is also a dwelling it opens out a clearing of truth and non-material significance that joins it to other ontological portals such as works of art.

"The mere object is not the work of art," Heidegger wrote in another influential essay that marks his later period of thought (final version 1950).[8] We might echo this by saying the mere structure is not the building. The humble nature of the hut might obscure its profound depth of meaning, its ability to allow thinking, preserving, and holding. Likewise, then, as we complexify and extend the project of building, so too does this project become complicated. Aesthetic elements are added, or rather interwoven, into function; the building demands time and space for us to see it. Some writers like to contrast this demand on our time with the one-glance-sees-all of paintings, but this does a disservice to visual art. Nevertheless, the durability and size of buildings is central to their existence. The floors offer affordances to the human form, and this must be reliable over time. A building must stand up, and it must also last—commodity, firmness, and delight as the Vitruvian adage has it, with firmness firmly bracketed.

In short, buildings are *meant for us* in intricate and looping ways. We build them but in essence they build us, forcing their way into the world through the minds, imaginations, and skills of human builders. They, like all of us who see and experience the building, do not wish simply to exist, they desire to *live*. Holding the hostile external world at bay is necessary yet insufficient. In addition, it cannot really achieve its own goal: the natural world comes inside with us, *as* us. The artifice of artful construction, as Harries describes Kafka's safety-seeking creature, is artificial in another, hidden yet obvious sense: security is an illusion.

And so we don't simply build to shelter, but also to speculate and remember.

Monuments are testaments, often compromised, to historical time. Follies are *memento mori*, the large-scale equivalents of the skull upon the desk in a Dutch still life. Ruination is as essential to post-Edenic condition as the quickness of living and breathing. *Et in Arcadio ego*, the budding artist Charles Ryder inscribes upon a human skull—purchased from the Oxford medical school—in Evelyn Waugh's *Brideshead Revisited* (1945). In this novel of memory, desire, regret and exultation—told entirely in retrospect—time itself emerges as the central character. Even the sturdy building at its heart, the country estate called Brideshead, does not emerge unscathed by the terrors of temporal passage. Of course it doesn't!

Et in Arcadia ego. The skull always lies beneath the skin, however dewy and flushed with pleasure, and Arcadia is a place from which we must always be expelled. And yet, there is nothing more human than to seek its pleasures again and again—and crucially for my purposes, to engage that quest in public. The grave may be a fine and private place, but before we go there we want something more than privacy.

It was Aristotle, in the *Nicomachean Ethics*, who first argued for the central role of leisure in human life, and for the idea of public spaces in which to pursue its special gifts. The Greek word he employed, *skholé*, has no exact English equivalent. It is retained as the root of *school*, but you would need time and some fancy intellectual footwork to convince schoolchildren that they are at leisure. "We work to have leisure," Aristotle says. It is the condition "on which happiness depends." Leisure, he elaborates, is "a state of being free from the necessity to labor." In his monumental *Politics*, the philosopher calls it "the first principle of all good action."

Clearly leisure means something quite different, on this account, from the typical understanding we accord to it. For us today, leisure might connote rest from work, yes, but almost always with an associated resonance of rest and recreation. Time off from work is still effectively colonized by work, since it is leisure in the service of restoring the worker's mental and physical fitness for the tasks of employment. Aristotle's leisure resembles cognate notions such as the Sabbath: this is time out of time, set off from workday principles and expectations. Here we are meant to contemplate the highest parts of ourselves, the divine presence within—or at least to set aside the cares and preoccupations of quotidian life in favor of a more transcendent form of activity.

We have to concede that leisure can often go off the rails, descending into mere idleness; unreflective boredom; and, worst of all, new forms of competitive consumption. Nothing is more depressing to witness than the perpetual races to the bottom of aggressive leisure: progressive "glamping" or cottage one-upmanship, on the one hand (who can make leisure more like a glossy magazine spread?), and by reversal, the hardship sweepstakes of extreme climbing, BASE-jumping, big-wave surfing, deep spelunking, and the like. One wants to intercede and say: *Everyone just relax! What you're doing is not leisure, it's just work by other means!*

* * *

How does all this relate to the simple hut and its extensions into more complex buildings and spaces? Well, let us think again of Aristotle's claim that genuine leisure is the basis of happiness because it calls out the best in our natures—the divine, ideally, if that doesn't sound too grand. Not working, or genuine leisure, is an activity without profit or reward that nevertheless remains in some sense productive. We are not merely twiddling our thumbs, we are *engaged*. Engaged in what? In some sense, that does not matter, as long as the engagement generates a passionate and invested response. Leisure should be viewed less as a particular activity and more as a way of *being at home in the world*.

That is of course the optimistic vision of the time out of time that philosophers imagine as true leisure. I won't speak further here of the many depredations of work and culture that colonize and hollow out this vision.[9] I am, rather, interested in what the seeking of leisure time in specific places—public spaces—means for us today.

We must be clear: if building itself, from the hut on up, was a way to try and conquer the existential terror of time, it is clear that the creation of enclosures also opened up new rifts and inversions in our seeking after diversion from death. We often speak of breaches into the domestic enclosure as "home invasion," setting out in linguistic form the sense of warfare—the return to natural conditions of might—that characterizes such violations of the private. But what of those moments when we choose to enter the public space, to spend the time that we have bought against our existential going in enjoyment of what we share, not just what we shelter?

In material terms, buildings rarely stand alone. A hut on a hillside in the *Schwarzwald* is one thing—a luxury good, in fact, a place of leisure for a privileged man who can play at earthly life in a manner not unlike Marie Antionette's notorious turns as a milkmaid at Versailles. For most of us, and all of us who live in cities and do not enjoy cottages or country homes, leisure time must be found elsewhere. True, there are many—perhaps too many—forms of "leisure" activity that are entirely domesticated. From backyard barbecues to bouts of video gaming in the TV room, one may choose not to leave the house when work is suspended. But still, the streets and squares beckon. They are, in one sense, simply the spaces created by the buildings around them. But more deeply, they are places of gathering and community, our version of the Athenian agora or the great central plazas of medieval towns. We leave the house, crossing the threshold from private to public, to find ourselves anew.

It is not just the space that is different when we venture into the public realm. Our sense of time, so often tied to work and the demands of capital, is freed to new possibilities. We walk more slowly, we tarry and laze, we are off the clock. The afternoon stretches before

us as a clear horizon, not an agonized duration of measured existence. We may even, if we are lucky, briefly slip the bonds of mortal
reckoning: not in reality, but in an oneiric state of transcendence that
is surely what Aristotle meant when he said that we touch the divine
in genuine leisure. In a French idiomatic slippage, we move from a
sense of confronting *la future*, that wall-like inevitable future of capital and technology, to dwelling in *l'avenir*—what will come.

We may seem, in the details of these six walks, to have ventured
a long way from the ethics of architecture. My contention, and my
compass reading, is that, to the contrary, we have ventured more
deeply into architecture's beating heart. A building may appear to
stand mute, a machine for living or working, a functional layering
of systems. It takes its place within an even more complex system
of technological, aesthetic, and commercial networks, negotiating
these and making its own particular contribution to the whole.

But a building is also, and always, an intimation of mortality, a
material reminder of the temporal fragility of human life. A great
building may well outlast a given individual lifetime, and some,
like the great French cathedrals, may take several human lifetimes
to realize their completion. These facts are at once triumphal and
chastening to the human spirit. How much more so, then, is the even
longer-term awareness that even the greatest and most monumental
building will someday fall into ruins, to become a folly or an aesthetic anomaly—the "ruin porn" of broken columns and crumbling
coliseums. I find myself, as I walk through a city layered with old and
new edifices, with a skyline spanning decades or even centuries, and
with deep strata of construction, destruction, and reconstruction literally paving my way, of Shelley's 1818 sonnet *Ozymandias*:

> I met a traveller from an antique land,
> Who said—"Two vast and trunkless legs of stone
> Stand in the desert. . . . Near them, on the sand,
> Half sunk a shattered visage lies, whose frown,
> And wrinkled lip, and sneer of cold command,
> Tell that its sculptor well those passions read
> Which yet survive, stamped on these lifeless things,

The hand that mocked them, and the heart that fed;
And on the pedestal, these words appear:
My name is Ozymandias, King of Kings;
Look on my Works, ye Mighty, and despair!
Nothing beside remains. Round the decay
Of that colossal Wreck, boundless and bare
The lone and level sands stretch far away.

Time makes servants of us all, cold-command sneer or not. That is inevitable, and it is indeed mockery, but only of the existential kind we can find everywhere around us, chiding our grandiose ambitions and fleeting obsessions. But how you govern yourself under these harsh conditions is ever the challenge of creative life, and indeed life more generally. When you hear the call of professional and individual conscience, when (as Heidegger avers) *Being* sounds its insistent ontological draw upon you, you must cut through the chatter of everydayness and answer.

Who you work for? In the end, that question turns out to be easy to answer, and yet exceptionally difficult to live up to. You work for posterity, of course, even knowing that it, too, is a demanding and sometimes capricious client. Just that, and that is everything. Meanwhile, be an everyday public hero. Cross thresholds even as you create them with your drafting stylus or desktop program. Dance to the music of time. Take time out of time for drifting through your city, your mind, your library, your culture. That is your calling; that is your vocation.

And above all, when in doubt: take a walk, or just *go outside and play!*

7
Epilogue: Afterthoughts, or Thoughts After Walking

My concern in this short perambulation within the ethics of architecture can be summed up with a postscript concerning the future.

Suppose the validity of the following three claims:

1: *play* is the phenomenological intersection of time, space, and place
2: we have entered a post-human, or cyborg, future of time, space, and place
3: cyborg environmentalism is the future of human (especially urban) life

What this could mean for the future of architecture is perhaps not immediately obvious, even if we accept that the three linked assertions are valid or anyway arguable. What is *cyborg environmentalism*?

What I imagine here is a form of building that takes into account the possibility of the technological singularity, whereby nonhuman intelligence surpasses the human form(s), but such that in future there will be trans-human and post-human options that avoid negative possible outcomes (human extinction, human isolation, human inferiority) and focus instead on the chance of human-non-human *integration*.[1]

Since part of the argument is that we are already highly integrated into nonhuman systems—phones and computers, but also buildings and environmental networks—further integration is likely and

The Ethics of Architecture. Mark Kingwell, Oxford University Press (2021). © Mark Kingwell.
DOI: 10.1093/oso/9780197558546.003.0008

desirable. We can execute integrative options gradually or all at once, but the desirability of pursuing integration as the most successful future outcome, for both human and nonhuman systems, seems obvious.

This is not utopian, but it is clearly a version of the "city of tomorrow" visions that have long clung to architectural practice and urban planning. We might want to discard the adjective "smart" from our accounts of integrated buildings, neighborhoods, and cities, but the ideal pushing innovation in built environments remains pretty constant: we want to *mesh*, not isolate or refuse. Even techno-skeptics of a certain neo-Luddite persuasion (I include myself among these) can see the potential benefits of closer and more fruitful integration. Neo-Luddism is not identical with technophobia; it is a corrective, not a refusal.

And so utopian thinking, or anyway anti-anti-utopian thinking, passes from the political (Plato's *Republic*, e.g., transformed by philosophy itself) to the physical (More's *Utopia*, e.g., transformed by going to another part of the map) to the temporal: the kinds of futures imagined by Le Corbusier in Modernism, or Constant Nieuwenhuys in Situationism. Which is to say, futures that are open-ended, democratic, playful, and aesthetically vivid. Here we can express the difference, preserved in French, between *le future* (the future as a brute inescapable fact) and *l'avenir* (an open sense of what is to come).

What this mean in terms of current and soon-to-come practice cannot always be readily described. There are urban projects that arrive with great fanfare, as already mentioned: Sidewalk Labs in Toronto, for example, or Hudson Yards in New York; but do these projects, which rely heavily on smartphone cross-tracking and surveillance, really count as environmental in the broader sense? The short-term future presumably holds out more options of this kind, but also, one hopes, more debate about the viability and wisdom of certain technologies, including triangulation, data gathering, and the Internet of Things.

Maybe more promising are integrations that respect the natural siting and conditions of local existence. This respect embraces everything from basic design to imagined program and choice of materials palette. It is already the case that architectural design is comprehensively technological—it is impossible to image the career of Frank O. Gehry absent the computer-generated designs necessary to create and execute his signature style—but in the future this kind of integration will likely expand and ramify, to good effect.

We should not fear the singularity, or the trans- and post-human futures that lie beyond it. This is the evolution of architecture in the broadest and most embracing sense: designing and building, forging form out of imagination and available technology. It was ever thus, and new technological possibilities mean new excitement.

As the science-fiction writer William Gibson has been quoted as saying, "The future is already here—it's just not very evenly distributed." Maybe the final ethical lesson we can take away from these perambulations is something like: Let's distribute the future more evenly, even if never perfectly. Who do you work for? You work for *everyone*, human or otherwise.

Acknowledgments

I would never have written about architecture in any capacity absent the example of Karsten Harries, of Yale University, who elevated my understanding of philosophical aesthetics and especially architectural theory *circa* 1989, when I was his graduate teaching assistant. At the time, I was an aspiring political theorist in the Hobbes-Locke-Kant-Rawls tradition. (That part of my training is no doubt still visible here.) Though he was not part of my doctoral committee, Professor Harries taught me that I should consider more than abstract liberal political philosophy in the built environment. Human life is bigger than thought experiments, and critical reflection should start in the street, not the seminar room.

I thank Markus Dubber, my colleague at the Centre for Ethics, University of Toronto, who pioneered this emerging series with Oxford University Press. Further thanks to Paul Vermeersch, visionary poet; Ken Greenberg, a generous presence in our shared city of Toronto; Wendy Pautz of LMN Architects, Seattle, and Maegan Magathan of Cornell University; George Baird, Larry Richards, An Te Liu, Richard Sommer, Robert Levit, John Shnier, and Mary Louise Lobsinger, at the Daniels Faculty of Architecture, Landscape, and Design, University of Toronto; and Joanne Tod, Edward Burtynsky, Matthew Pillsbury, Kent Monkman, Shelagh Keeley, Blue Republic, Bruno von Ulm, Lisa Klapstock, Stephen Appleby-Barr, Ross Racine, John Hartman, and James Lahey for aesthetic inspiration.

I am grateful to three anonymous readers at Oxford University Press for their comments and to OUP series editor Jamie Berezin, for his care and attention. I acknowledge special debts to the partners and associates at KPMB Architects, Toronto, especially Bruce Kuwabara, Marianne McKenna, Shirley Blumberg, Geoffrey Turnbull, and Amanda Sebris. Invitations to lecture at their offices over the last several years have focused and refined my ideas.

Finally, I thank the students and faculty I have been privileged to meet during more than twenty-five years of teaching at the University of Toronto; Cambridge University; the University of California at Berkeley; the University of Chicago; Baruch College in the City University of New York; and the Faculdade de Arquitetura e Urbanismo, Escola da Cidade in São Paulo. They have always made me see things anew. Various public and academic audiences in North America, Europe, the Middle East, Australia, and Asia have also informed and improved my thinking about cities and buildings.

Some portions of this book were previously published, in earlier form, as the following: "Monumental/Conceptual Architecture," *Harvard Design Magazine* 19 (Fall 2003/Winter 2004); "Building, Dwelling, Acting," in Graham Owen, ed., *Architecture, Ethics and Globalization* (New York: Routledge, 2009), pp. 40–49;

"The Politics of Risk," *LA+ Risk* (Fall 2017): pp. 6–11; "Fugitive Democracy: A Gift in Time," in Renée Köhler-Ryan, ed., *Living the Catholic Tradition: Philosophical and Theological Considerations* (Steubenville, OH: Franciscan University Press), pp. 195–232; and "Public Space and the Terrorism of Time," in Vikas Mehta, ed., *Companion to Public Space* (New York: Routledge, 2020), pp. 429–37. The section of Chapter 2 on interiors and affordances was written at the behest of Andrew Furman and Jay Irizawa of the Ryerson University School of Interior Design, Toronto, for a possible anthology. I am grateful to all the editors for their interest in my work.

This book is dedicated to my mother, Gertrude Pauline Kingwell (1938–2019).

Notes

Preface: Plague Cities of the Future

1. Timothy Findley, *Headhunter* (Toronto: HarperCollins, 1993), p. 8.
2. Ibid., p. 216. There are other apposite details: conspiracist rumors that the virus has been spawned by a lab accident, for example, and then covered up with government complicity; and dark, quasi-fascistic rhetoric about "a new social contract" emerging in the wake of contagion.
3. Sample quotation: "If and when the WFH-ers [work-from-homers] do head back in, the office life they once knew will likely be gone, replaced by largely empty floors, with few if any meetings and elevator rides, and everyone in masks." See Maxwell Strachan, "You're Not Going Back to Normal Office Life for a Long, Long Time," *Vice* (April 22, 2020); https://www.vice.com/en_us/article/5dm7pk/youre-not-going-back-to-normal-office-life-for-a-long-long-time
4. One of these developments, Toronto's nineteen-building St. James Town, is just a few blocks from where I live. One of the nation's most crowded districts, the site of two major recent fires, the area has long been considered a blight on Toronto's record of urban planning: "Residents live in cramped conditions, in many cases sharing apartments. They are surrounded by a ragged quilt of parking lots, garage ramps and beat-up lawns. A community centre, library and elementary school are the only good public spaces. There's one threadbare public park. Yet these 19 high-rise buildings are home to at least 15,000 people—nobody knows exactly how many—of whom more than half are immigrants and roughly two-thirds are visible minorities. Roughly one-third rent from Toronto Community Housing, and the rest from private landlords."

    In 2020, the impossibility of social distancing added to the district's long-standing afflictions. See Alex Bozikovic, "In the Pandemic, Toronto's St. James Town Needs Room to Breathe," *The Globe and Mail* (April 22, 2020); https://www.theglobeandmail.com/canada/toronto/article-in-the-pandemic-torontos-st-james-town-needs-room-to-breathe/
5. Katherine Kersten, "Density in a Time of Coronavirus: Do You Trust Your 'New Urbanist' Overlords?," *Minneapolis Star Tribune* (April 3, 2020); https://www.startribune.com/katherine-kersten-density-in-a-time-of-coronavirus/569364112/. A reply was offered by Kate Wagner, "Don't Blame Dense Cities for the Spread of Coronavirus," *Curbed* (April 22, 2020); https://www.curbed.com/2020/4/22/21224935/coronavirus-density-debate-mcmansion-hell-kate-wagner.

Also by Carol Galante, "Now Is The Time to Embrace Density," *New York Times* (May 12, 2020); https://www.nytimes.com/2020/05/12/opinion/urban-density-inequality-coronavirus.html.

Galante's argument was essentially directed by positive urban externalities: density offers a more just distribution of opportunities than sprawl: "The further threat is that the pandemic becomes a rallying cry to maintain our sprawling fortress neighborhoods designed to foster exclusion rather than inclusion. We have an obligation to ignore the short-term reactionary impulse to blame density for the spread of the coronavirus and instead use this opportunity to rethink the policies that impede the construction of new housing, at more price levels, in the places where housing is most needed."

6. João Pina, as told to Nina Strochlic, "Living Inside Brazil's Largest Apartment Complex amid a Pandemic," *National Geographic* (April 16, 2020); https://www.nationalgeographic.com/history/2020/04/living-inside-brazil-largest-apartment-complex-amid-coronavirus-pandemic/

7. Sabrina Tavernise and Sarah Mervosh, "America's Biggest Cities Were Already Losing Their Allure. What Happens Next?," *New York Times* (April 19, 2020); https://www.nytimes.com/2020/04/19/us/coronavirus-moving-city-future.html. The *Times* later dialed up their assessment of future cities in a brilliant online/print essay, focused especially on inequality in cities (complete with required quotation from Plato's *Republic*), in an essay by its Editorial Board, "The Cities We Need," *New York Times* (May 11, 2020); https://www.nytimes.com/2020/05/11/opinion/coronavirus-us-cities-inequality.html.

8. Oliver Wainwright, "Smart Lifts, Lonely Workers, No Towers or Tourists: Architecture After Coronavirus," *The Guardian* (April 13, 2020); https://www.theguardian.com/artanddesign/2020/apr/13/smart-lifts-lonely-workers-no-towers-architecture-after-covid-19-coronavirus.

9. Compare Alex Bozikovic, "The COVID City: Disease Shaped Architecture in the 20th Century. Will It Do That Again?," *Globe and Mail* (May 2, 2020); https://www.theglobeandmail.com/arts/art-and-architecture/article-the-covid-city-disease-shaped-architecture-in-the-20th-century-will/

Likewise see Ken Greenberg, "Crises of the Past Century Brought Great Advances. Will COVID-19 Help Create a New Kind of City?," *Toronto Star* (May 3, 2020); https://www.thestar.com/opinion/2020/05/03/crises-of-the-past-century-brought-great-advances-will-covid-19-help-create-a-new-kind-of-city.html

Introduction

1. Lance Hosey, "*The Fountainhead*: Everything That's Wrong With Architecture," *Architecture Daily* (November 14, 2013); https://www.archdaily.com/447141/the-fountainhead-everything-that-s-wrong-with-architecture

2. "Facing Up to the Future: Prince Charles on 21st Century Architecture," *The Architectural Review* (December 20, 2014); https://www.architectural-review.com/essays/facing-up-to-the-future-prince-charles-on-21st-century-architecture/8674119.article

3. Douglas Murphy, "Prince Charles's 10 principles for architecture— and 10 much better ones," *The Guardian* (December 27, 2014); https://www.theguardian.com/artanddesign/2014/dec/27/prince-charles-10-principles-architecture-10-better-ones

4. Ibid.

5. Katie Rogers and Robin Pogrebin, "Draft Executive Order Would Give Trump a New Target: Modern Design," *New York Times* (February 5, 2020). "The order, spearheaded by the National Civic Art Society, a nonprofit group that believes contemporary architecture has 'created a built environment that is degraded and dehumanizing,' would rewrite the current rules that govern the design of office buildings, headquarters, and courthouses, or any federal building project contracted through the General Services Administration that costs over $50 million." Further: " 'For too long architectural elites and bureaucrats have derided the idea of beauty, blatantly ignored public opinions on style, and have quietly spent taxpayer money constructing ugly, expensive, and inefficient buildings,' Marion Smith, the group's chairman, wrote in a text message. 'This executive order gives voice to the 99 percent—the ordinary American people who do not like what our government has been building.' " Yay, beauty—with columns and pediments!

6. A number of distinguished thinkers have tackled this question. Without pretending to exhaustiveness, see Karsten Harries, *The Ethical Function of Architecture* (Cambridge, MA: MIT Press, 1996); Gregory Palermo, Patrick Sullivan, and Barry Wasserman, *Ethics and the Practice of Architecture* (Hoboken, NJ: Wiley, 2000); Warwick Fox, ed., *Ethics and the Built Environment* (New York: Routledge, 2000); Thomas Fisher, *The Architecture of Ethics* (New York: Routledge, 2018); and *Ethics for Architects* (Princeton, NJ: Princeton Architectural Press, 2010); Tom Spector's *The Ethical Architect* (Princeton, NJ: Princeton Architectural Press, 2000). My hope with the present volume is to build on these essential texts, in perhaps briefer form and with a more specific focus on my own specialties, justice theory and practical ethics.

7. Ken Greenberg, personal conversation, Toronto, December 13, 2019. Strict grammarians would say that it should be "whom do you work for," but the basic rhetorical power of idiom prevails here, as it should.

8. Michael Sorkin, "Two Hundred and Fifty Things an Architect Should Know," *Reading Design* (March 31, 2020); https://www.readingdesign.org/250-things. Also included in Sorkin, *What Goes Up* (London: Verso, 2018).

Chapter 1

1. Translator Frederick Etchells not only altered the text, using the thirteenth French edition; he also inserted the adjective "new" into the title without permission (New York: Dover, 1986; facsimile of London: John Rodker, 1931).

2. Mark Kingwell, *Nearest Thing to Heaven: The Empire State Building and American Dreams* (New Haven, CT: Yale University Press, 2006).

3. Mark Kingwell, *Concrete Reveries: Consciousness and the City* (New York and Toronto: Viking/Penguin, 2008).

4. *The Singularity* was first explored by mathematician and physicist John von Neumann and later taken up in more detail by, among others, mathematician and science-fiction author Vernor Vinge, in his essay "The Coming Technological Singularity: How to Survive in the Post-Human Era" (NASA Technical Reports, 1993). The "singular" part, often misunderstood, is that once there is just one nonhuman algorithm capable of self-reproduction and possible learning and improvement, there is a very steep acceleration curve of nonhuman "intelligence." A good philosophical consideration is David Chalmers, "The Singularity: A Philosophical Analysis," *Journal of Consciousness Studies* 17 (2010): pp. 7–65. See also Ray Kuzweil, *The Singularity Is Near: When Humans Transcend Biology* (New York: Penguin, 2006).

5. See, for a sampling, the following links.

   From 2016, a general overview: Rron Bequiri, "A.I. Architecture Intelligence," *Future Architecture* (May 4, 2016); http://futurearchitectureplatform.org/news/28/ai-architecture-intelligence/

   From 2018, a five-point update: Donovan Alexander, "5 Ways Artificial Intelligence Is Changing Architecture," *Interesting Engineering* (December 8, 2018); https://interestingengineering.com/5-ways-artificial-intelligence-is-changing-architecture

   And from 2019, the inevitable article arguing that AI will put much of the profession out of business: Marcus Fairs, "Rise of Artificial Intelligence Means Architects Are 'Doomed', Says Sebastian Errazuriz," *Dezeen* (October 22, 2019); https://www.dezeen.com/2019/10/22/artificial-intelligence-ai-architects-jobs-sebastian-errazuriz/

6. https://thefunambulist.net/law/militarized-architectures-the-evil-architects-do-by-eyal-weizman; https://www.thenewatlantis.com/publications/the-architecture-of-evil

7. See, for example, Richard Sennett, *Building and Dwelling: Ethics for the City* (New York: Farrar, Straus and Giroux, 2018).

8. Some of these ideas were first explored as part of the Fourth Harrison Symposium on Professionalism, at the Tulane University School of Architecture in New Orleans (March 2000). The symposium took as its theme "Architecture, Ethics, and Globalization." It therefore encouraged a larger scope on the idea of ethics

beyond mere professional responsibility. My thanks go to Graham Owen for the invitation, and for giving the symposium such an interesting direction. I would also like to acknowledge fellow participants Ellen Dunham-Jones, Geoffrey Galt Harpham, Janice Newson, and Garry Stevens for challenging comments that, in many cases, prompted important revisions of my thinking. Part of section 4 of the paper was previously published in the magazine *Adbusters* (June/July 2000) as a column called "Long Live the New Flesh."

9. The image of the architect-as-wizard, disdainful and aloof, is a recurring problem for the profession of architecture, not least because it is such an attractive role for aspiring members of the profession. It is also an important cog in the machine of architecture's reputation, part of the allure. Garry Stevens's book *The Favored Circle: The Social Foundations of Architectural Distinction* (Cambridge, MA: MIT Press, 1998) is an extended sociological analysis, after the manner of Pierre Bourdieu's notion of symbolic capital exchange, on how the profession continues this economy of influence. So thus Pierre Bourdieu, "The Forms of Capital," in J. G. Richardson, ed., *Handbook of Theory and Research for the Sociology of Education* (New York: Greenwood Press, 1986), pp. 241–58.

10. Martin Heidegger, "Building Dwelling Thinking," in *Poetry, Language, Thought*, trans. Albert Hofstadter (New York: Harper & Row, 1971), pp. 143–62.

11. I have written elsewhere about the failure of Modernism's emancipatory political promise in the sprawl of the Potsdamer Platz. See Mark Kingwell, "Style," *Azure* (November/December 1998), pp. 41–43; and reprinted in *Marginalia: A Cultural Reader* (Toronto: Penguin, 1999), pp. 25–30.

12. Peter Conrad, *Modern Times, Modern Places* (New York: Knopf, 1999); I have here borrowed a number of details from Conrad's superb analysis of modernism.

13. See Mark Kingwell, *Wish I Were Here: Boredom and the Interface* (Montreal and Kingston: McGill-Queen's University Press, 2019).

14. Walter Benjamin, *The Arcades Project*, trans. Howard Eiland and Kevin McLaughlin (Cambridge, MA: Harvard University Press, 1999). If the prospect of curling up with a book almost 1,100 pages long gives you pause, you might prefer to read just my review essay of it, "Arcadian Adventures," *Harper's Magazine* (March 2000): pp. 70–76. For more on the idea of "post-cultural" identity, see Christopher Clausen, "Nostalgia, Freedom, and the End of Cultures," *Queen's Quarterly* (Summer 1999): pp. 233–44.

15. For more on the role of despair in Plato's political philosophy, and the crucial issues of isomorphism between the individual and surrounding sociocultural environment, see Jonathan Lear, "Inside and Outside the Republic," in his collection of essays, *Open Minded* (Cambridge, MA: Harvard University Press, 1998), pp. 219–46. Lear's psychoanalytic interpretations of the standard Platonic and Aristotelian texts reveal new layers of meaning crucial to a sufficient mindfulness of our limitations in political theory (or anything else).

16. Mark Kingwell, "The Dream House," *Azure* (July/August 1999): pp. 32–34; and Terence Riley, "The Un-Private House" (New York: Museum of Modern Art, January 6, 1999). See also the classic text in the field, Gaston Bachelard, *The Poetics of Space*, trans. Maria Jolas (Boston: Beacon Press, 1969).

17. Donna Haraway, "A Cyborg Manifesto: Science, Technology, and Socialist Feminism in the Late Twentieth Century," *Socialist Review* 15:2 (1985). Included in her collection *Simians, Cyborgs, and Women: The Reinvention of Nature* (New York: Routledge, 1991), pp. 149–81.

18. The Occupy Wall Street protests began in Zuccotti Park, Manhattan, on September 17, 2011, and quickly spread to many cities around North America and the world. The slogan "We are the 99 percent" was a rallying cry against the increasing concentration of wealth in the highest percentile edges of the global population. My co-author Joshua Glenn and I were pleased to see that our little book *The Idler's Glossary* (Windsor, ON: Biblioasis, 2008), designed and decorated by the brilliant artist Seth, was part of the free-circulation Occupy Library, a collection of subversive books that was later trashed by New York City police when the Occupy protest was broken up.

19. Walter Benjamin, *One-Way Street and Other Writings*, trans. Edmund Jephcott and Kingsley Shorter (London: Verso, 1979).

20. Hannah Arendt, in *The Human Condition* (Chicago: University of Chicago Press, 1958), divides human effort into three categories: labor, work, and action. The first, *labor*, is concerned with meeting basic human biological needs, such as a food, clothing, and shelter. This first realm is closely aligned with Aristotle's notion of the realm of necessity. *Work* concerns creation, usually of a specific end-directed (teleological) goal and employing tools: a house, for example, or even just a table or chair. Only *action* then qualifies as public life, the region of political identity and citizenship. It is a central contention of this walk and this book that work can, perhaps must, be a form of action.

21. Rem Koolhaas, *Delirious New York: A Retrospective Manifesto for New York* (New York: Monacelli Press, 1974; Oxford: Oxford University Press, 1978). Later editions of the book, such as the 1994 Monacelli reissue, instead feature two sleek Modernist towers on the cover (but not the World Trade Center, as is often assumed).

22. Alpha Rho Chi is still a professional fraternity for architecture students and "the allied arts." Better than Sigma Chi, those charmless goons on campuses hither and yon. Chi Rho, meanwhile, is for pharmacists. I have no idea what that means, if anything.

Chapter 2

1. This odd cultural association drawn between a building that *seems to dance* with a famous Hollywood dance couple must make us recall the famous dictum,

attributed to everyone from David Byrne, Frank Zappa, and Elvis Costello to Brian Eno and Thelonius Monk, that "writing about music is like dancing about architecture." The usual gloss on this bit of critical wisdom is that the latter is obviously fatuous and absurd, and therefore so is the former. Let music be music, critics and academics! Sheesh. But, having written a fair bit about music, I feel like the poles ought to be reversed here. Which is to say: Why *shouldn't* we dance about architecture? In fact, isn't that what we do every single day, as we spin through revolving doors like pirouetting ballerinas, glide down corridors like tangoing Valentinos, or dash into elevators like rough-and-tumble Gene Kelly hoofers?

2. The thought appears, appropriately, in Pascal's *Pensées*, first published in 1669, but has become an often-quoted commentary, usually moralistic in tendency, on contemporary phone-enabled immersion in stimulation. I will suggest, per Heidegger, that the problem at hand is not technology as object (the phone) but technology the ideology (comprehensive consumption of the world, including the self).

3. I expand on these brief thoughts concerning thresholds, especially in relation to urban spaces and their phenomenological effects and opportunities, in Mark Kingwell, *Concrete Reveries: Consciousness and the City* (New York: Viking, 2008).

4. J. J. Gibson, "The Theory of Affordances," ch. 8 of his book *The Ecological Approach to Visual Perception* (Boston: Houghton Mifflin, 1979). There is now a vast literature on affordances, especially in design, which I will not attempt cite here. Note that some affordances consist of explicit instructions (the "Push" sign on a door) while others rest as subtle or contextual "invitations" for interaction. Note, too, that affordances are distinct from the properties of objects: an antique bone china teacup may possess the property of fragility without that affecting its ability to offer an opportunity for drinking. Other vessels, with other properties, might offer the same opportunity. Product design may be defined, in one sense, as the interaction between these two aspects.

5. Here I am paraphrasing some of the same arguments I make in a longer consideration of tables and chairs—under the sign of "a philosophy of furniture"—in my essay "Tables, Chairs, and Other Machines for Thinking," in Mark Kingwell, *Practical Judgments: Essays on Politics, Culture, and Interpretation* (Toronto: University of Toronto Press, 2002). Compare architectural-social theorist Wytold Rybczynski, *Now I Sit Me Down: From Klismos to Plastic Chair: A Natural History* (New York: Farrar, Straus & Giroux, 2016).

6. Martin Heidegger, *Being and Time* (*Sein und Zeit*, 1927), trans. John Macquarrie and Edward Robinson (London: Blackwell, 1962).

7. The canonical article is Andy Clark and David J. Chalmers, "The Extended Mind," *Analysis* 58:1 (January 1998): pp. 7–19.

8. Martin Heidegger, *The Fundamental Concepts of Metaphysics: World, Finitude, Solitude*, trans. William McNiell and Nicholas Walker (Bloomington: Indian University Press, 1995), pp. 343–44.

9. See Marshall McLuhan, *Understanding Media: The Extensions of Man* (New York: McGraw-Hill, 1964).

10. See Martin Heidegger, "The Question Concerning Technology," in *The Question Concerning Technology and Other Essays*, trans. William Lovitt (New York: Garland, 1977).

11. Ibid., p. 35.

12. Aldo Rossi, *The Architecture of the City*, trans. Diane Ghirardo and Joan Oakman (Cambridge, MA: MIT Press, 1984).

13. Shaftesbury, *Characteristics of Men, Manners, Opinions, Times* (orig. 1711), especially Section II of Book III. Characteristic argument: "[T]here is nothing so divine as BEAUTY: which belonging not to *Body*, nor having any Principle or Existence except in MIND and REASON, is alone discover'd and acquir'd by this diviner Part, when it inspects it-self, the only object worthy of itself." (A. Ashley-Cooper, *Characteristics* [Indianapolis: Liberty Fund, 2011], p. 238.)

14. Zoe Craig, "11 Secrets of London's Eros Statue," *Londonist* (2016); https://londonist.com/london/history/secrets-of-the-eros-statue.

15. Alicia Keys, Randy Newman, Serge Gainsbourg, John Cale, Eminem, Elvis Costello, The Beastie Boys, PJ Harvey, Galaxie 500, The Fabulous Thunderbirds, etc. etc.

16. Kingwell, *Nearest Thing to Heaven*, op. cit.

17. Walter Benjamin, *The Arcades Project*, trans. Howard Eiland and Kevin McLaughlin (Cambridge, MA: Belknap Press, 2002); and cf. Michel Foucault, *Discipline and Punish: The Birth of the Prison*, trans. Alan Sheridan (New York: Pantheon Books, 1977).

Chapter 3

1. See, for example, the work of Thomas Homer-Dixon, beginning with a landmark article called "Environmental Scarcities and Violent Conflict: Evidence from Cases," *International Security* 19:1 (1994): pp. 5–40. This was later followed by both a general-audience overview in *The Atlantic* and a book, *Environment, Scarcity, and Violence* (Princeton, NJ: Princeton University Press, 2001).

2. An excellent philosophical discussion of the nuances here can be found in Neil Levy, "Autonomy and Addiction," *Canadian Journal of Philosophy* 36:3 (2006): pp. 427–47, especially 432 and 431. I discuss these issues in specific relation to technology in Kingwell, *Wish I Were Here*, op. cit.

3. Andy Borowitz, "Trump Economic Plan Calls for Every American to Inherit Millions From Father," *New Yorker* (August 8, 2016).

4. John Rawls, *A Theory of Justice* (Cambridge MA: Belknap Press, 1970). My characterization is crude but I hope not inaccurate for present purposes. For further reflections on the basics of the theory and its relation to chance, see

Mark Kingwell, "Throwing Dice: Luck of the Draw and the Democratic Ideal," *PhaenEx* 7:1 (2012): pp. 66–100; reprinted in Mark Kingwell, *Unruly Voices* (Windsor, ON: Biblioasis, 2012).

5. Nikhil Naik, Scott Duke Kominers, Ramesh Raskar, Edward L. Glaeser, and César A. Hidalgo, "Computer Vision Uncovers Predictors of Physical Urban Change," *PNAS Early Edition* (November 2017).

6. James Q. Wilson and George L. Kelling, "Broken Windows," *The Atlantic Monthly* (March 1982). This theory built on arguments introduced by Oscar Newman, *Defensible Space: Crime Prevention Through Urban Design* (New York: Macmillan, 1973), analyzing the role of architecture and urban design in respect of safety and community trust.

7. One very talented architecture student I knew back at this time was asked to design a "shopping centre," which she did by burying the main wedge-shaped structure underground and having one tiny entrance above ground. I imagine most people find depressing the ubiquitous suburban vernacular of the strip mall, with varied small retail outlets—restaurant, nail salon, electronics store— set off from a main drag by a small parking area; but I'm not sure that a bunker-like buried mall is a preferable option.

8. Oliver Wainwright, "The Despot Dilemma: Should Architects Work for Repressive Regimes?," *The Guardian* (January 27, 2020).

Chapter 4

1. Le Corbusier, *Towards a New Architecture*, ed. cit., p. 37.

2. Ibid., p. 3.

3. Ibid., pp. 25, 37.

4. Witold Rybczynski, *The Look of Architecture* (New York: Oxford University Press, 2001), p. xii.

5. Ibid., p. xiv.

6. Le Corbusier, *Towards a New Architecture*, ed. cit., p. 3.

7. Michael Wright and Dania Herrara, "Decline and Fall—Evelyn Waugh versus Modernism (1928)," *Modernist Tourists* (2016); https://modernisttourists.com/2016/08/04/decline-and-fall-evelyn-waugh-versus-modernism-1928/

8. Manifestos have not gone anywhere. Recent examples in the world of design alone include Jessica Helfand's *First Things First Manifesto* (2000) and Bruce Mau's much-reprinted (and much-mocked) *Manifesto for Incomplete Growth* (1998). Full disclosure: I myself published what I called "a sort-of manifesto" in favor of male dandyism in 2001 (*Journal X* 5:1–2 [Spring]: pp. 151–67).

9. Witold Rybczynski, "A Discourse on Emerging Tectonic Visualization and the Effects of Materiality on Praxis: Or an Essay on the Ridiculous Way Architects Talk," Slate (February 2, 2011); https://slate.com/culture/2011/02/architecture-speak-an-essay-on-the-ridiculous-way-architects-talk.html

10. See, for example, Melony Ward and Bernie Miller, eds., *Crime and Ornament: The Arts and Popular Culture in the Shadow of Adolf Loos* (Toronto: YYZ Books, 2002). Also Hal Foster, *Design and Crime (And Other Diatribes)* (New York: Verso, 2002), especially chs. 2 and 4. Bruce Mau, Rem Koolhaas, and Frank Gehry come in for particularly effective drubbings at Foster's hands.

11. The Deutscher Werkbund was an association of craftspeople, artists, architects, and designers established in 1907. Its ambit was the creation of affordable and well-designed objects and buildings suitable for the new century and its democratization of aesthetics. There is a close tie here to Bauhaus. One might have thought Loos would be sympathetic here, but his argument is that the Werkbund is not wrong but *unnecessary*—a state-sponsored trade organization, however well meaning, cannot determine style; only the epoch can do that.

12. Adolf Loos, "Ornament and Crime," in Ulrich Conrads, ed., *Programs and Manifestos on 20th Century Architecture* (Cambridge, MA: MIT Press, 1975), p. 20.

13. Ibid.

14. Ibid.

15. The best commentary on this troubled relationship between politics and aesthetics remains Benjamin's landmark 1935 essay, "The Work of Art in the Age of Mechanical Reproduction," trans. Harry Zohn, in Hannah Arendt, ed., *Illuminations* (New York: Schocken Books, 1969), pp. 219–26. If anyone was "forever on the run" it was Benjamin, who fled Berlin for Paris, and then Paris for the Spanish Frontier, where he perished by his own hand in 1940.

16. Henry Grosshans, *Hitler and the Artists* (New York: Holmes & Meier, 1983), p. 86. It might be noted here, parenthetically, that both the art world in general and *New York itself* have been considered inherently Jewish, elite, and degenerate: "Jew York City," as creepy white supremacists like to say.

17. Arthur Danto, "The Museum of Museums," in *Beyond the Brill Box: The Visual Arts in Post-Historical Perspective* (Berkeley: University of California Press, 1992), pp. 199–216.

18. Bedford is described online as "a senior editor at *The Federalist*, the vice chairman of Young Americans for Freedom, a board member at the National Journalism Center, and the author of *The Art of the Donald*," whatever that might be. Okay, for you, I looked it up: it is a self-help book whose full title is *The Art of the Donald: Lessons from America's Philosopher-in-Chief* (New York: Threshold Editions, 2017). There is, alas, no licensing function on the use of the term "philosopher" in public discourse, though experience indicates it should always be approached with caution.

19. Christopher Bedford, "Behind the White House Move to Stop Ugly Federal Buildings (and the Architects Who Stand in the Way," The Federalist (February 7, 2020); https://thefederalist.com/2020/02/07/behind-the-white-

house-move-to-stop-ugly-federal-buildings-and-the-architects-who-stand-in-the-way/

20. See Tom Wolfe, *From Bauhaus to Our House* (New York: Farrar, Straus & Giroux, 1981).

21. Brianna Rennix and Nathan J. Robinson, "Why You Hate Contemporary Architecture (and if You Don't, Why You Should)," *Current Affairs* (October 31, 2017); https://www.currentaffairs.org/2017/10/why-you-hate-contemporary-architecture. Worth noting, perhaps, that the writers are graduates of the Harvard and Yale law schools, and as of this writing are in their early 30s.

22. Douglas Adams, *The Long Dark Tea-Time of the Soul* (London: Heinemann, 1988). It is relevant to point out that this musing is part of the free indirect discourse of a fictional character, the "holistic" detective Dirk Gently.

23. Heather Mallick, "Our Cities Are Ugly and We Know Who to Blame," *Toronto Star* (February 24, 2020); https://www.thestar.com/opinion/star-columnists/2020/02/24/our-cities-are-ugly-and-we-know-who-to-blame.html

24. Martin Heidegger, "On Origin of the Work of Art [*Der Urpsrung des Kunstwerkes*, 1950]," in David Farrell Krell, ed., *Basic Writings* (New York: Harper Collins, 2008), pp. 143–212.

25. P. J. O'Rourke, *Holidays in Hell* (New York: Grove Atlantic, 1988).

26. See, for example, Kingwell, "Concrete's Softer Side," *Saturday Night Magazine* (June 3, 2000): pp. 64–67. This short appreciation of concrete was the origin of my 2008 book *Concrete Reveries*, ed. cit.

27. For a clear, occasionally slightly technical, early primer on mass timber, see Hallie Busta, "Mass Timber 101: Understanding the Emerging Building Type," *Construction Dive* (May 24, 2017); https://www.constructiondive.com/news/mass-timber-101-understanding-the-emerging-building-type/443476/

28. Indeed, against the banal strip-mall or big-box ambitions of shopping-mall clients, the aforementioned underground design was intended as a critique of their very existence and, incidentally, of their capitalist philistinism. That is not a good way to build a practice, but it does possess intellectual and aesthetic integrity, of a purebred elitist sort.

29. Jason Farago, "Beyond Architecture, A Builder of Lusty Fantasies," *New York Times* (February 6, 2020); https://www.nytimes.com/2020/02/06/arts/design/Lequeu-Morgan-Library.html?action=click&module=Features&pgtype=Homepage

30. Robert Venturi, Steven Izenour, and Denise Scott Brown, *Learning from Las Vegas: The Forgotten Symbolism of Architectural Form* (Cambridge, MA: MIT Press, 1972). The distinction defended here by the authors is between "ducks"—buildings that signify their function or intention via explicit form (the paradigm is an egg-retail franchise shaped in the form of a duck) and other buildings that adapt basic "decorated shed" forms to their purpose via external additions and explicit signage. Of course the distinction is highly tendentious, if not untenable.

At what point does a decorated shed become an organic duck-like signal of its function? And why, after all, should function be communicated in direct, kindergarten-level forms? A good brief commentary may be found in Kurt Kohlstedt, "Lessons from Sin City: The Architecture of 'Ducks' Versus 'Decorated Sheds,'" *99% Invisible* (September 26, 2016); https://99percentinvisible.org/article/lessons-sin-city-architecture-ducks-versus-decorated-sheds/

Chapter 5

1. https://living-future.org/just/
2. http://justorganizations.com/content/organizations
3. Note, for example, Elsa Lam, editor of *Canadian Architect* magazine, who observes that "millennials are also interested in addressing the climate crisis and equity-related issues, and in seeing the positive impacts of their work. They want to make places that bring together communities, that help socially and economically marginalized people around the globe, and that contribute positively to the environment. As a generation, they hope to turn around the wrongs they see in the world" (*Canadian Architect*, July 2019, p. 4). One can take issue with the very idea of "millennials" as a distinct category of people, but this observation does reflect a sense of demonstrable shift when it come to architectural practice, much of it age-based.
4. For more on this issue and its relation to the notion of *tradition*—Chesterton's stated concern in the quotation included here—see Mark Kingwell, "Fugitive Democracy: A Gift in Time (Revised)," in Renée Köhler-Ryan, ed., *Living the Catholic Tradition: Philosophical and Theological Considerations* (Steubenville, OH: Franciscan University Press, 2019), pp. 195–232.
5. See John Rawls, *A Theory of Justice* (Cambridge, MA: Belknap Press, 1971 and 1999), especially section 44; Rawls, *Political Liberalism* (New York: Columbia University Press, 1993), p. 274; Rawls, *Justice as Fairness: A Restatement* (Cambridge, MA: Belknap Press, 2001), especially sections 49.2 and 49.3.
6. Rawls, *Political Liberalism*, p. 274; Rawls, *Justice as Fairness*, p. 160.
7. I won't attempt to cite the whole body of criticism here. A telling early response was Kenneth J. Arrow, "Rawls's Principle of Just Saving," *Swedish Journal of Economics* 75:4 (December 1973): pp. 323–35; compare the later concerns expressed in Thomas Schramme, "Is Rawlsian Justice Bad for the Environment?," *Analyse & Kritik* 28 (2006): pp. 146–57.
8. Chesterton was an indefatigable controversialist—his own age's Christopher Hitchens, perhaps—and he cannot resist jibes at contemporaries. My (unfair) favorite: "Surely one might pay for extraordinary joy in ordinary morals. Oscar Wilde said that sunsets were not valued because we could not pay for sunsets. But Oscar Wilde was wrong; we can pay for sunsets. We can pay for them by

not being Oscar Wilde." G. K. Chesterton, *Orthodoxy* (orig. 1905; Peabody, MA: Hendrickson, 2006), p. 53. All further quotations are taken from this edition.

9. Ibid., ed. cit., p. 43.
10. Ibid., p. 43.
11. Ibid., p. 43.
12. Ibid., pp. 96, 116, and 30–31.
13. Ibid., p. 137.
14. A good brief overview of the dispute is offered by Anthony Paletta, "Story of Cities #32: Jane Jacobs v Robert Moses, Battle of New York's Urban Titans," *The Guardian* (April 28, 2016); https://www.theguardian.com/cities/2016/apr/28/story-cities-32-new-york-jane-jacobs-robert-moses
15. In addition to Jacobs's classic, National Book Award-winning work *The Death and Life of American Cities* (New York: Vintage, 1991; orig. 1961), there is the monumental Pulitzer Prize-winning biography of Moses by Robert A. Caro, *The Power Broker: Robert Moses and the Fall of New York* (New York: Knopf, 1974); Anthony Flint's *Wrestling with Moses: How Jane Jacobs Took On New York's Master Builder and Transformed the American City* (New York: Random House, 2011); and Roberta Brandes-Gratz, *The Battle for Gotham: New York in the Shadow of Robert Moses and Jane Jacobs* (New York: Nation Books, 2010). There is even an opera for this operatic clash of titans, probably a first in its subject matter: *A Marvelous Order* (music by Judd Greenstein, libretto by Tracy K. Smith, 2016 *et seq.*).
16. Adam Gopnik, "Why They Bulldozed Your Neighbourhood," *The New Yorker* (October 21, 2019); https://www.newyorker.com/magazine/2019/10/28/why-they-bulldozed-your-block. The book under review in Gopnik's essay is Lizabeth Cohen, *Saving America's Cities: Ed Logue and the Struggle to Renew Urban American in the Suburban Age* (New York: Farrar, Straus & Giroux, 2019).
17. Charles Taylor, *Modern Social Imaginaries* (Durham, NC: Duke University Press, 2004), p. 96.
18. Ibid., p. 97.
19. Lewis Mumford, *Technics and Civilization* (Chicago: University of Chicago Press, 2010), p. 17.
20. F. W. Taylor, *The Principles of Scientific Management, in The Early Sociology of Management and Organizations, Vol. 1: Scientific Management* (New York: Routledge, 2005), p. 129. Compare Rem Koolhaas, *Delirious New York*, ed. cit., which relates Taylor's time-motion ideas to the spectacular rise of first-generation skyscrapers in Manhattan, especially the Empire State Building, as discussed previously.
21. Guy Debord, *Society of the Spectacle*, sec. V:126.
22. But see Mark Kingwell, "The Work Idea: Wage Slavery, Bullshit, and the Good Infinite," in Todd Dufresne and Clara Sacchetti, eds., *The Economy as Cultural*

System: Theory, Capitalism, Crisis (New York: Bloomsbury, 2013), pp. 127–40; reprinted in *Unruly Voices*, ed. cit., at pp. 181–96 and as the Introduction to Kingwell and Joshua Glenn, *The Wage Slave's Glossary* (Windsor, ON: Biblioasis, 2011).

23. Witold Rybczynski's *Waiting for the Weekend* (New York: Viking, 1991) tells a gripping version of this story, set against the Babylonian origin of the seven-day week itself.

24. Martin Heidegger, "The Age of the World Picture," in trans. William Lovitt, *The Question Concerning Technology and Other Essays* (New York: Harper & Row, 1977).

25. Guy Debord, *Society of the Spectacle*, sec. V:145.

26. E. P. Thompson, "Time, Work-Discipline, and Industrial Capitalism," *Past & Present* 38 (1967): pp. 69, 90.

27. Taylor, *Modern Social Imaginaries*, op. cit., p. 157.

28. Ibid., p. 110.

29. Bruce Ackerman, *We The People, Volume I: Foundations* (Cambridge, MA: Belknap Press, 1991) and *Volume II: Transformations* (Cambridge, MA: Belknap Press, 2000).

30. A. Bartlett Giamatti, *Take Time for Paradise: Americans and Their Games* (New York: Summit Books, 1989), p. 44.

31. I thank Diana Boros for introducing the notion of *buy-outs* to my thinking about wealth and public space. "As economic inequality has only continued to grow in the twenty-first century, class divisions in America are more and more visible, particularly in our public spaces," she writes. "Generally speaking, the wealthier an individual, the more likely they are to be able to 'buy themselves out' of truly public experiences. . . . [I]t is too often the situation that the public spaces that have been ignored by the privileged soon become neglected. So not only do we collectively lose the vital experiences of diverse interaction, but also the spaces themselves" (personal correspondence).

32. The *Citizens United v. Federal Election Commission* decision of the United States Supreme Court (558 U.S. 310 [2010]) is an example of how an otherwise democratic nation can consume itself from within, a version of Derrida's "auto-immunity." The decision grants money the status of political speech, therefore under protection of the First Amendment to the U.S. Constitution. This makes it possible for the wealthy to exercise massive force multipliers on their political views, since money now literally talks.

Chapter 6

1. Guy Debord, *Society of the Spectacle* [*La société du spectacle*] (orig. 1967; Detroit, MI: Black & Red, 1983), *passim*. Also Lewis Mumford, *Sidewalk Critic: Lewis*

Mumford's Writings on New York, ed. Robert Wojtowicz (New York: Princeton Architectural Press, 2000).

2. Andy Martin, "The Incel Rebellion—How Involuntary Celibates Are Dangerous in Their Desires," *The Independent* (May 4, 2018); https://www.independent.co.uk/news/long_reads/incel-what-is-involuntary-celibates-elliot-rodger-alek-minassian-canada-terrorism-a8335816.html.

3. Karsten Harries, "Building and the Terror of Time," *Perspecta: The Yale Architecture Journal* 19 (1982): p. 59; see also Mark Kingwell, "Public Space and the Terrorism of Time," in Vikas Mehta, ed., *Companion to Public Space* (New York: Routledge, 2020).

4. Harries, "Building and the Terror of Time," p. 59.

5. Ibid., p. 60.

6. Pamela Furdin, "A Nantucket Hermit Is Pulled from His Shell," *Washington Post* (December 29, 1998); https://www.washingtonpost.com/archive/politics/1998/12/29/a-nantucket-hermit-is-pulled-from-his-shell/07b85d7c-f887-41ab-8f89-f8b263592cf2/?utm_term=.d81b52782c16

7. Martin Heidegger, "Building Dwelling Thinking," in *Poetry, Language, Thought*, ed. cit.

8. Martin Heidegger, "The Origin of the Work of Art," in *Poetry, Language, Thought*, ed. cit.

9. See Mark Kingwell, "Idling Toward Heaven: The Last Defence You Will Ever Need," *Queen's Quarterly* 115:4 (Winter 2008): pp. 569–85; also the Introduction to Kingwell and Joshua Glenn, *The Idler's Glossary* (Windsor, ON: Biblioasis, 2008).

Chapter 7

1. I explore the philosophical issues raised here in a forthcoming book, *Singular: The Ethics and Politics of Posthuman Life* (Montreal and Kingston: McGill-Queen's University Press, 2022).

Index

materials, 5, 43–44, 80–83, 113–14. *See also specific topics*
media, 83–84
mimesis is not mimicry, 6
Minassian, Alek, 110
mind–body problem, 45, 54
misfortune, 58–59, 61
modern art, 75
modernism, xviii, 71–72, 73, 74, 78
    modes of, 15–16
modernist aesthetic movements, 15–16
modernist movement, German, 75
modernity, 22–23, 24, 25
monuments, 51–54, 118
moral architect, 8
moral ideal, 8–9
"morality," 1
    vs. ethics, 9–10
    translations of the term, 9
Moses, Robert, xvi, 93–95
Mumford, Lewis, 97, 109
Murphy, Douglas, 4–5
    Prince Charles and, 4–5, 6
    principles for architecture, 5–7
music, 135n1

narrative of origin, 101–2
natural environment, limits of
    the, 31–32
nature, 7, 112–13. *See also* environment
    culture and, 31
    humankind and, 7, 32–33
    mastery of, 32–33
    state of, 101, 112
Nazi Germany, 74–76
    aesthetics and, 74, 75
    art and, 75–76
Neal, Patricia, 3
neighborhoods, 18–19, 57,
    64–65, 94, 95
neoclassical designs, 75, 80
neoliberalism, xi, 62
Nice truck attack (2016), 110
9/11 terrorist attacks, xiv, 82–83
Nouvel, Jean, 67

Objectivism, 7. *See also Fountainhead*;
    Rand, Ayn
Occupy Wall Street, 134n18
open-plan house, 47–48
open spaces, 106
Order-One Risk, 58, 59, 62, 64
Order-Three Risk, 62, 63–64
Order-Two Risk, 59–60, 62
original position, 61–62, 90, 101. *See
    also* veil of ignorance
O'Rourke, P. J., 81–82
"Ozymandias" (Shelley), 121

painting(s), 80–81, 84
pandemics, ix. *See also* plagues
    wealth and, xi
Parker House in Boston, 51
parks, xviii–xix
Pascal, Blaise, 42–43, 135n2
pedestrians, 5, 111
Plague, The (Camus), xiv–
Plague City, ix
plague condition, architectural
    contours of the city as part of
    the, xvi
plagues, xiv–xv. *See also* pandemics
plastic media, 84
Plato, 17, 37–38, 102, 134n15
Plato's Cave, 102
play, 59, 122, 123
politics
    aesthetics and, 16, 17, 18, 75,
        138n15
    global/globalized, 20
    post-evolutionary, 31–32
    post-human future, 123, 125
    postmodernism, 25–26
power. *see also under* Charles, Prince
        of Wales
    wealth and, 25–26, 60, 98–99
privacy, xx, 48
private realm, 30–31, 34–35, 104,
    105. *See also* public space: vs.
    private space
professional ethics, 10–11, 72, 96